NAME

SHARPEN YOUR SKILLS

Numbers and Their Purposes

Write what kind of number to use in each situation.

1. Counting the number of cars in a parking lot

2. Finding a radio station on the dial

3. Determining the number of people who attended a movie

4. Finding a city on a state map

5. Cutting a pie into equal pieces

6. Comparing the prices of apples and oranges

7. Comparing the number of spectators who prefer basketball to tennis

8. Recording the finish times of swimmers in hundredths of seconds

9. Finding a point on a graph

10. Comparing the speed of a car with the speed of an airplane

NAME

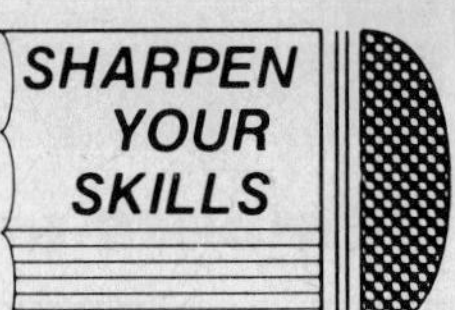

Number Sense in Measurement

Choose the most sensible unit to express each measurement.

1. The time it takes you to go from your home to school

____

2. How hot the hot water from your tap is

____

3. The length of your shoe

____

4. The time it takes to run 100 yards

____

5. The length of the school year

____

6. The distance from Peoria, Illinois to Cleveland, Ohio

____

7. The length of a truck

____

8. The time of Christopher Columbus until now

____

Estimation Estimate an appropriate temperature.

9. Hot soup

____

10. Ice cold lemonade

____

Complete each sentence with a sensible unit of measurement.

11. The distance from Los Angeles to New York City is about 2,800 ______.

____

12. A car can travel about 55 miles per ______ on the highway. Therefore a car could travel about 550 ______ in 10 hours.

____

Use after pages 6–7.

NAME ______________

SHARPEN YOUR SKILLS

First Quadrant Graphing

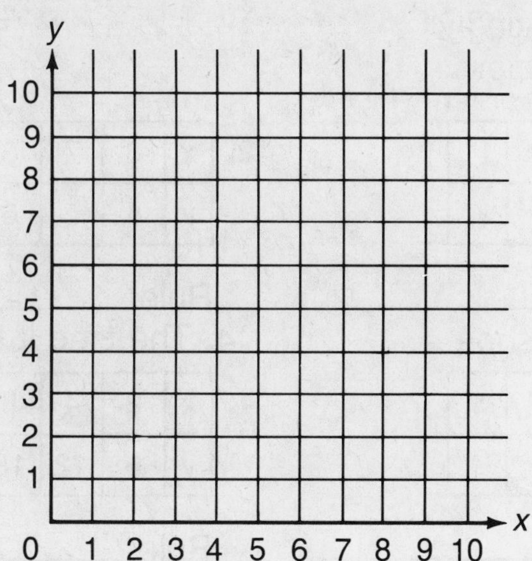

Graph and label these points on the grid.
Remember to move along the *x*-axis first.

1. A (2, 4) **2.** B (2, 2) **3.** C (1, 6) **4.** D (4, 7) **5.** E (3, 5)

6. F (0, 8) **7.** G (6, 7) **8.** H (9, 3) **9.** I (4, 5) **10.** J (8, 4)

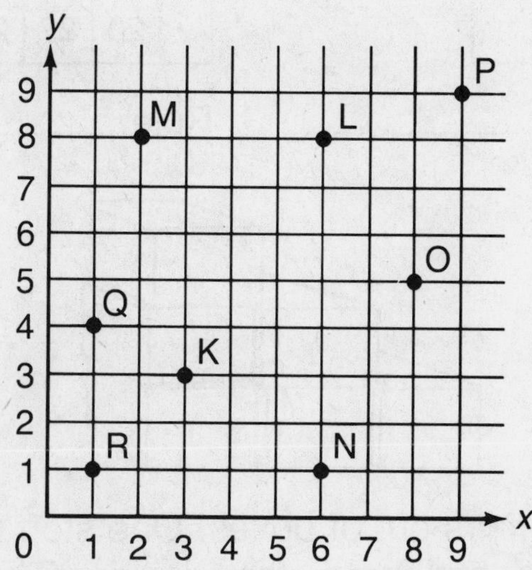

Write the coordinates of each point.

11. K ________ **12.** L ________ **13.** M ________ **14.** N ________

15. O ________ **16.** P ________ **17.** Q ________ **18.** R ________

NAME

SHARPEN YOUR SKILLS

Number Patterns: Tables

Find the rule for calculating *y*.
Then complete each table.

1.

x	1	3	5	7	9	11
y	5	7	9			

Rule: ______________________

2.

x	6	7	8	9	10	11
y	4	5	6			

Rule: ______________________

3.

x	3	4	5	6	7	8
y	12	16	20			

Rule: ______________________

4.

x	2	4	6	8	10	12
y	6	12	18			

Rule: ______________________

5.

x	6	8	10	12	14	16
y	3	4	5			

Rule: ______________________

6.

x	3	7	8	5	10	21
y	2	6	7			

Rule: ______________________

7.

x	2	3	4	5	6	7
y	17	18	19			

Rule: ______________________

8.

x	10	11	12	13	14	15
y	20	22	24			

Rule: ______________________

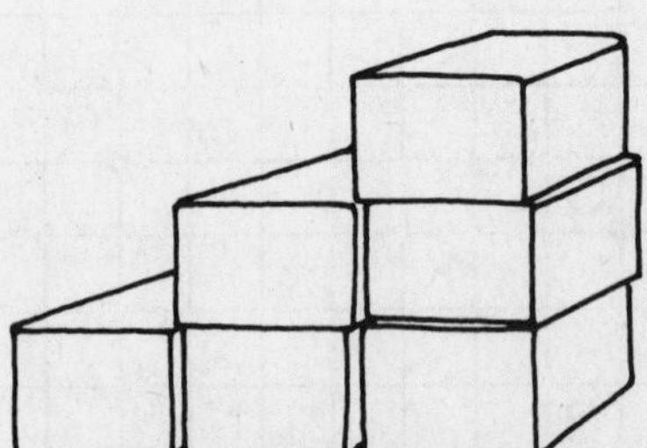

Solve.

John is building a set of stairs out of boxes. One step requires 1 box, two steps require 3 boxes, and three steps require 6 boxes.

9. How many boxes will he need to make 4 steps?

____

10. How many boxes will he need to make 10 steps?

____

NAME

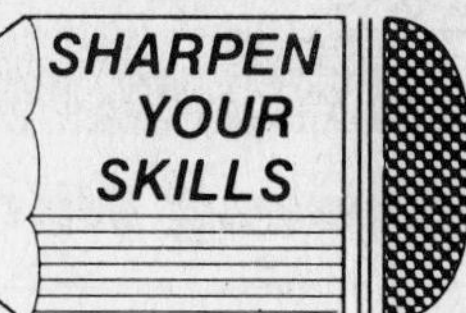

Using A Problem-Solving Guide

Solve each problem. Use the Problem-Solving Guide to help you.

1. Two hikers walk all summer. One of them travels 503 miles, and the other travels 497 miles. What is the total distance walked by the two hikers?

2. What is the difference between the distances the two hikers walked during the summer?

3. Three families traveled by car around the United States during the summer. The Hughes family drove 2,765 miles, the Davidsons drove 3,678 miles, and the Quinlans drove 4,094 miles. What is the total distance the three families drove?

4. The Rubens family drove 1,007 more miles than the other three families together. How far did they travel?

5. Caroline had such a good time at camp last summer that she could hardly wait to go back. In fact she decided to figure out how many hours it would be until she would return. She counted exactly 7 weeks and 6 days. How many hours did she have to wait?

6. When Caroline found out how many hours she had to wait, she wanted to know how many minutes this would be. She could imagine the lake and how much fun she would have. How many minutes did she have to wait?

NAME

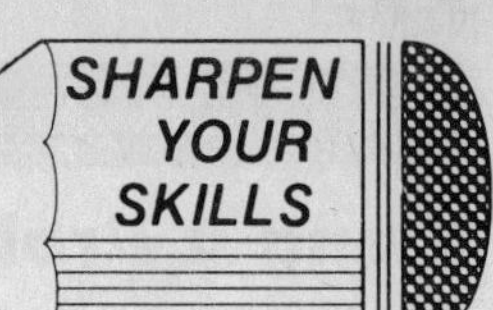

Naming Whole Numbers and Decimals

Write each number in words.

1. 73,000,207,000

2. 54,093,540,000,210

3. 790,276,431

4. 6.482

5. 90.231

6. 413.027

7. 73.78007

8. 2.900087

9. 34.4939

Write each number in standard form.

10. eight trillion, six billion, five hundred thousand, two

11. six hundred trillion, fifty billion, twenty million, three thousand

12. six hundred seventy-two millionths

13. six hundred and seventy-two millionths

NAME

Comparing and Ordering Whole Numbers and Decimals

Compare these numbers. Use >, <, or =.

1. 17.563 ◯ 23.855

2. 89,771 ◯ 79,999

3. 89,441 ◯ 89,911

4. 28.167 ◯ 28.167

5. 19,522 ◯ 20,413

6. 62.248 ◯ 62.193

7. 86.471 ◯ 86.471

8. 10,000 ◯ 1,000

List the numbers in order from least to greatest.

9. 8,241 8.258 8,293 ____________________

10. 6.023 6,004 6.099 ____________________

11. 67,812 67,218 67,716 ____________________

12. 67 6,792 679 67,928 ____________________

13. 528.979 524.112 528.003 ____________________

Solve the problems.

14. Max and Susan worked a number puzzle. Max completed the puzzle in 50.25 seconds and Susan in 50.19 seconds. Who took longer?

____

15. Andrea ran the 100-yard dash in 11.98 seconds. Pam ran it in 11.96 seconds. Who won the race?

____

Use after pages 16–19.

NAME

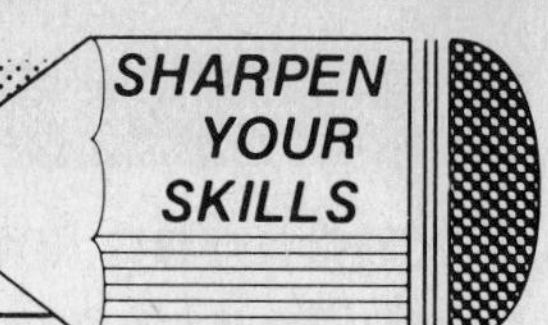

Rounding Whole Numbers and Decimals

Round to the nearest whole number.

1. 8.7 ____________ **2.** 4.2 ____________ **3.** 9.5 ____________

4. 21.5 ____________ **5.** $4.94 ____________ **6.** $8.06 ____________

Round to the nearest tenth.

7. 0.92 ____________ **8.** 0.47 ____________ **9.** 4.17 ____________

10. 8.66 ____________ **11.** 2.982 ____________ **12.** 3.314 ____________

Round to the nearest hundredth.

13. 0.431 ____________ **14.** 0.227 ____________ **15.** 0.944 ____________

16. 3.127 ____________ **17.** 1.109 ____________ **18.** 9.588 ____________

Round to the nearest thousandth.

19. 6.3294 ____________ **20.** 9.3225 ____________ **21.** 2.7003 ____________

Round 4,587,328,472 to the nearest

22. million ____________ **23.** billion ____________ **24.** thousand ____________ **25.** hundred ____________

26. ten ____________ **27.** ten-thousand ____________ **28.** ten million ____________ **29.** hundred-thousand ____________

NAME

SHARPEN YOUR SKILLS

Estimating Sums and Differences

Estimate each sum or difference. First round to the nearest whole number.

1. 5.4 + 7.2 ______

2. 17.8 + 26.2 ______

3. 9.799 + 4.23 ______

4. 6.7 − 5.6 ______

5. 321.3 − 20.9 ______

6. 49.234 − 39.9 ______

7. \$2.97 + \$3.59 ______

8. \$4.25 + \$9.15 ______

9. \$27.53 + \$17.79 ______

10. \$35.67 − \$6.17 ______

11. \$40.29 − \$8.55 ______

12. \$81.16 − \$19.61 ______

13. \$29.94 + \$14.53 + \$3.83 ______

14. \$410.00 + \$534.79 + \$45.16 ______

15. \$316.45 + \$15.76 + \$189.99 ______

16. Estimate the sum and the difference for Exercises 3 and 6 by rounding to the nearest tenth.

______

17. In Exercises 13 and 14, use front-end digits to give a range for each sum.

______

Use after pages 24–27.

NAME

SHARPEN YOUR SKILLS

Adding Whole Numbers and Decimals

Work each exercise and circle its answer in the chart below. Keep working exercises in any order until you have five in a horizontal, diagonal, or vertical line.

1. 27.3 + 184.35

2. 20.009 + 48.922

3. 116.2 + 0.095

4. 9.006 + 22.61

5. 549.7 + 4.123

6. 3.009 + 82.06

7. 321.66 + 86.37

8. 21.03 + 18.99

9. 6.589 + 37.007 = ________

10. 40.907 + 15.09 = ________

11. 711.01 + 12.402 = ________

12. 61.001 + 23.231 = ________

13. 721.3 + 10.095 = ________

14. 16.229 + 11.112 = ________

15. 13.067 + 15.267 = ________

16. 63.230 + 1.603 = ________

17. 195.97 + 206.37 = ________

18. 184.35 + 48.921 = ________

212.06	723.412	41.23	68.931	233.271
64.833	43.596	55.997	31.616	85.619
85.069	39.42	731.395	27.341	84.232
165.28	211.65	68.025	116.295	28.334
553.823	408.03	402.34	173.446	40.02

NAME

Subtracting Whole Numbers and Decimals

Estimate. Then subtract. **Remember** to align the decimal points before you subtract. The number in the center is the minuend.

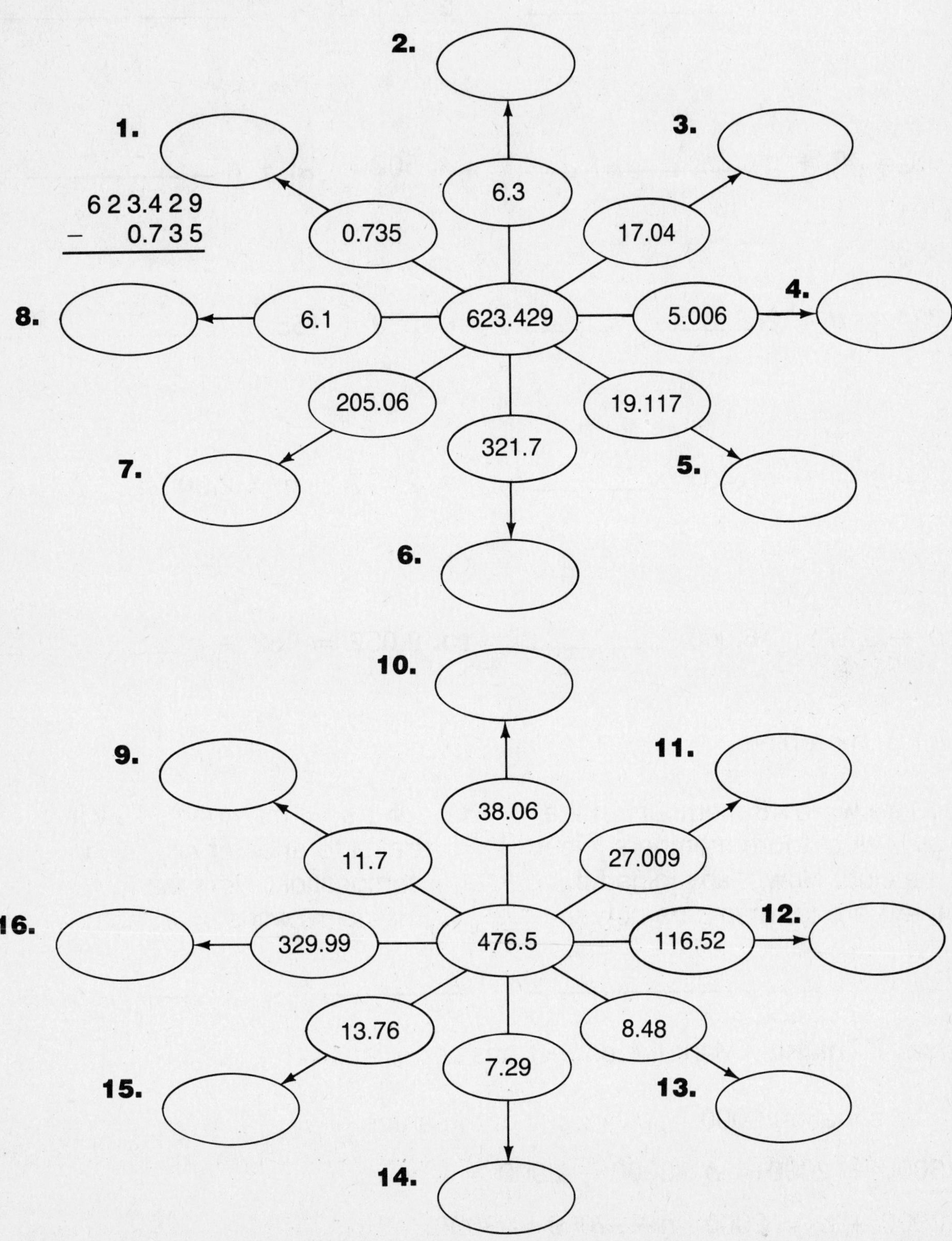

NAME

SHARPEN YOUR SKILLS

Solving Equations

Solve each equation.

1. $53 + n = 82$ __________

2. $n + 27 = 71$ __________

3. $63 = 47 + n$ __________

4. $502 = 42 + n$ __________

5. $734 = n + 258$ __________

6. $282 = 155 + n$ __________

7. $1{,}406 + n = 8{,}431$ __________

8. $2{,}477 + n = 2{,}903$ __________

9. $n + 3{,}274 = 6{,}000$ __________

10. $8{,}052 = 962 + n$ __________

Solve each problem.

11. There were 48 members in the gym club. More members joined the club. How many joined if there are 56 members now?

____

12. Of the 56 members, 15 will travel to another city for a competition. How many members will stay at home?

____

Critical Thinking Mark the correct answer or answers.

13. The equation $3000 = n + 2000$ is the same as

$3000 + 2000 = n$ $3000 - 2000 = n$

$3000 + n = 2000$ $n + 2000 = 3000$

Use after pages 32–33.

NAME

SHARPEN YOUR SKILLS

Write an Equation

Write an equation. Then solve each problem.

1. Steve has the lead in the school play. He studied his lines for 185 minutes on Tuesday and Wednesday. He studied for 98 minutes on Tuesday. How long did he study on Wednesday?

____

____

2. There were 120 tickets printed for Thursday's performance and 135 tickets for Friday's performance. How many tickets were printed for the two performances?

____

____

3. Karen bought 63 yards of cotton for the costumes. In all, 125 yards are needed for the costumes. How many yards does she still need to buy?

____

____

4. There are 67 costumes needed for the play. There were 32 costumes made in a week. How many more costumes need to be made?

____

____

5. At first, 12 students were selling tickets. Later 5 others joined to sell tickets. How many students were then selling tickets?

____

____

6. Joan has 75 programs to sell. She has sold 59 programs. How many programs does she still have to sell?

____

____

NAME

SHARPEN YOUR SKILLS

Multiplying by a One-Digit Multiplier

Multiply.

1. 19×6
2. 45×8
3. 821×9
4. 487×7
5. 409×4
6. 670×2
7. 33×6
8. 58×5

Find the missing number. Tell which property is shown.

9. $7 \times 61 = 61 \times$ ______ ____________________

10. $9 \times (3 \times 5) =$
$(9 \times$ ______$) \times 5$ ____________________

11. Complete the multiplication wheel. (Multiply each number by the number in the center. Put the answer in the appropriate space on the wheel.)

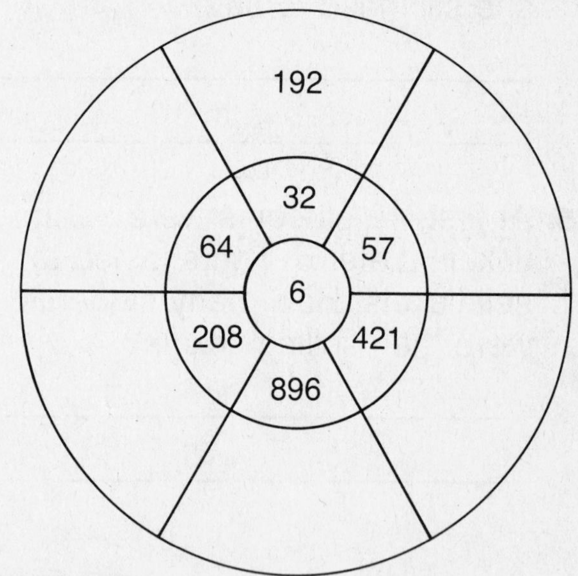

12. Give the sum of the numbers in the outside ring of the wheel.

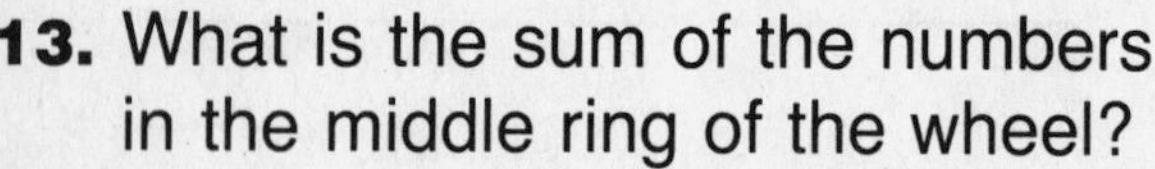

13. What is the sum of the numbers in the middle ring of the wheel?

____

14. What is the product when the answer to exercise 13 is multiplied by 6? ____________________

NAME

SHARPEN YOUR SKILLS

Exponents and Powers

Write each product using exponents and in standard form.

1. $7 \times 7 \times 7 \times 7 =$ ______ **2.** $6 \times 6 \times 2 \times 2 =$ ______

3. $5 \times 5 \times 9 \times 9 =$ ______ **4.** $8 \times 8 \times 11 =$ ______

5. $4 \times 4 \times 4 \times 4 \times 4 =$ ______ **6.** $2 \times 2 \times 2 \times 2 \times 7 =$ ______

What do you call a sad canary?

To find out, connect the star beside each exercise to the star beside its answer. Each line will go through a letter. Write the letter on the blank.

Exercise				Answer	
7. 8^3	★		★	243	______
		(E) (A)			
8. 4^2	★	(B)	★	144	______
9. 3^5	★		★	256	______
10. 9^3	★		★	72	______
		(L)			
11. 4^4	★	(I)	★	512	______
		(D)			
12. $3^2 \times 4^2$	★	(B)	★	50	______
13. $2^2 \times 5^2$	★		★	16	______
14. 2×5^2	★	(U)	★	100	______
15. $2^3 \times 3^2$	★		★	729	______

NAME

SHARPEN YOUR SKILLS

Patterns with Exponents

Write each number in expanded form using exponents.

1. 632 = ______

2. 1,883 = ______

3. 430 = ______

4. 2,507 = ______

5. 40,309 = ______

Write each number in standard form.

6. $(7 \times 10^4) + (3 \times 10^3) + (6 \times 10^2) + (5 \times 10^1) + 0 =$ ______

7. $(5 \times 10^3) + (2 \times 10^2) + (5 \times 10^1) + 6 =$ ______

8. $(6 \times 10^4) + (9 \times 10^2) + (6 \times 10^1) =$ ______

9. $(1 \times 10^5) + (3 \times 10^3) + (3 \times 10^2) + (1 \times 10^1) + 3 =$ ______

What famous character in a movie said, *"I am the night."*

To find out, connect the star beside each exercise to the star beside its answer. Each line will go through a letter. Write the letter on the blank.

10. $(1 \times 10^3) + (2 \times 10^2) + 4 =$ ______ ☆

11. $(4 \times 10^2) + (9 \times 10^1) + 4 =$ ______ ☆

12. $(5 \times 10^5) + (5 \times 10^2) =$ ______ ☆

13. $(7 \times 10^4) + (6 \times 10^3) + 1 =$ ______ ☆

14. $(8 \times 10^3) + (8 \times 10^2) =$ ______ ☆

15. $(1 \times 10^4) + (2 \times 10^1) + 2 =$ ______ ☆

Ⓙ Ⓞ Ⓣ Ⓐ Ⓚ Ⓑ Ⓐ Ⓔ Ⓝ Ⓜ Ⓡ

☆ 8,800 ____

☆ 500,500 ____

☆ 1,204 ____

☆ 10,022 ____

☆ 494 ____

☆ 76,001 ____

NAME

SHARPEN YOUR SKILLS

Mental Math: Multiples of 10

Multiply. Use mental math.

1. $6 \times 500 =$ ______

2. $400 \times 7 =$ ______

3. $40 \times 60 =$ ______

4. $50 \times 80 =$ ______

5. $30 \times 500 =$ ______

6. $700 \times 300 =$ ______

7. $4{,}000 \times 20 =$ ______

8. $90 \times 6{,}000 =$ ______

Show how you could use the distributive property to solve these problems mentally.

9. $4 \times 102 =$ ______

10. $7 \times 69 =$ ______

11. $5 \times 199 =$ ______

12. $2 \times 117 =$ ______

13. $6 \times 81 =$ ______

14. $9 \times 111 =$ ______

Use the distributive property to multiply mentally.

15. $5 \times 24 =$ ______

16. $3 \times 18 =$ ______

17. $2 \times 18 =$ ______

18. $7 \times 15 =$ ______

19. $3 \times 41 =$ ______

20. $9 \times 60 =$ ______

21. $4 \times 33 =$ ______

22. $8 \times 62 =$ ______

23. $6 \times 47 =$ ______

24. $7 \times 36 =$ ______

25. $9 \times 84 =$ ______

26. $5 \times 99 =$ ______

NAME

SHARPEN YOUR SKILLS

Estimating Products

Estimate the product by rounding each factor so that only the first digit is not zero.

1. 58 × 93 ______ **2.** 99 × 89 ______

3. 64 × 534 ______ **4.** 376 × 42 ______

Estimate the product by finding a range.

5. 67 × 938 ______ ______ **6.** 48 × 434 ______ ______

7. 32 × 756 ______ ______ **8.** 527 × 663 ______ ______

Estimate the product by using compatible numbers.

9. 5 × 32 ______ **10.** 439 × 11 ______

11. 102 × 13 ______ **12.** 6,156 × 93 ______

Estimate the answer to each problem.

13. A farmer hired 32 workers to pick watermelons. If each worker picked 76 watermelons, estimate how many watermelons were picked in all.

______

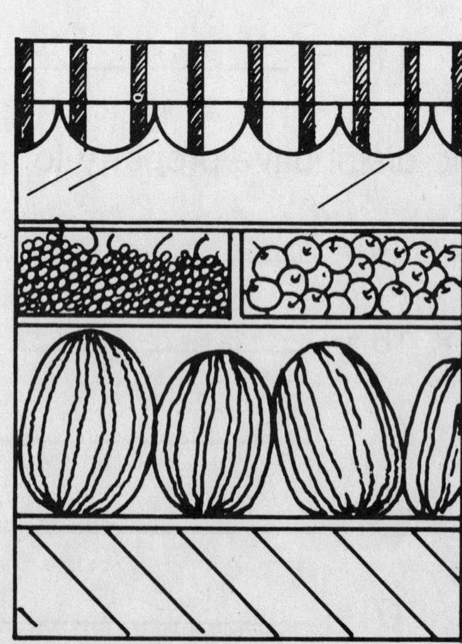

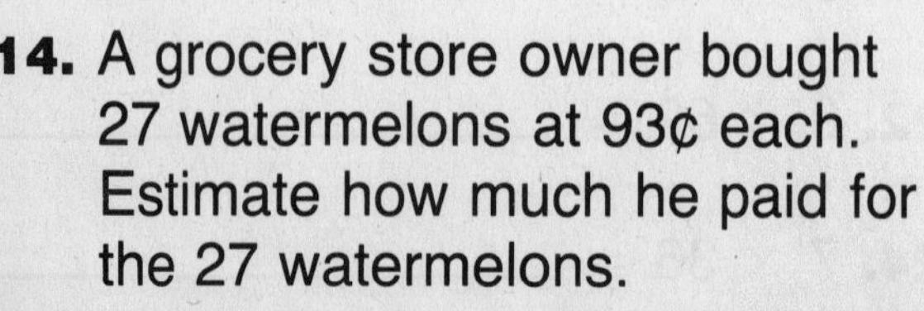

14. A grocery store owner bought 27 watermelons at 93¢ each. Estimate how much he paid for the 27 watermelons.

______

Use after pages 54–57.

NAME

SHARPEN YOUR SKILLS

Multiplying by Multiples of 10 or 100

Multiply.

1. $\begin{array}{r} 73 \\ \times 60 \\ \hline \end{array}$

2. $\begin{array}{r} 48 \\ \times 50 \\ \hline \end{array}$

3. $\begin{array}{r} 92 \\ \times 20 \\ \hline \end{array}$

4. $\begin{array}{r} 39 \\ \times 70 \\ \hline \end{array}$

5. $\begin{array}{r} 206 \\ \times 90 \\ \hline \end{array}$

6. $\begin{array}{r} 118 \\ \times 30 \\ \hline \end{array}$

7. $\begin{array}{r} 876 \\ \times 60 \\ \hline \end{array}$

8. $\begin{array}{r} 488 \\ \times 30 \\ \hline \end{array}$

9. $\begin{array}{r} 57 \\ \times 200 \\ \hline \end{array}$

10. $\begin{array}{r} 301 \\ \times 600 \\ \hline \end{array}$

11. $\begin{array}{r} 744 \\ \times 300 \\ \hline \end{array}$

12. $\begin{array}{r} 63 \\ \times 900 \\ \hline \end{array}$

13. 87 × 90 = ______________

14. 308 × 60 = ______________

15. 629 × 70 = ______________

16. 2,708 × 60 = ______________

Solve each problem.

17. A welder earns $15 an hour. How much does she earn in 40 hours?

____

18. A mechanic is paid $245 a week. How much does he earn in 20 weeks?

____

NAME

SHARPEN YOUR SKILLS

Multiplying by a Multi-Digit Number

Multiply. Be sure to estimate first and then compare with the actual product.

1. 54 × 21 = ________

2. 43 × 211 = ________

3. 35 × 109 = ________

4. 82 × 5,407 = ________

5. 1,624 × 228 = ________

6. 4,365 × 168 = ________

7. 63 × 8,724 = ________

8. 562 × 876 = ________

9. 72 × 1,048 = ________

10. 398 × 642 = ________

Mixed Practice Multiply.

11. 8 × 200 = ________

12. 9 × 6,418 = ________

13. 53 × 28 = ________

14. 442 × 64 = ________

15. 60 × 6,280 = ________

16. 487 × 12 = ________

17. 420 × 24 = ________

18. 989 × 62 = ________

Critical Thinking Look at Exercises 1-18. Write the numbers of the problems whose estimated products:

- result from a rounded factor of 100. ________
- result from a rounded factor of 200. ________
- result from a rounded factor of 1,000. ________
- result from a rounded factor of 6,000. ________

NAME

SHARPEN YOUR SKILLS

Choose a Computation Method

Tell whether you would use mental math, paper and pencil, or a calculator. Then find each answer.

1. $\begin{array}{r} 4{,}538 \\ +2{,}779 \\ \hline \end{array}$

2. $\begin{array}{r} 30 \\ \times\ 9 \\ \hline \end{array}$

3. $\begin{array}{r} 482 \\ -\ 56 \\ \hline \end{array}$

4. $\begin{array}{r} 75 \\ -25 \\ \hline \end{array}$

5. $\begin{array}{r} 550 \\ +\ 67 \\ \hline \end{array}$

6. $\begin{array}{r} 1{,}420 \\ \times\ 37 \\ \hline \end{array}$

7. 400 × 43 = ____________

8. 3,909 + 6,574 = ____________

9. 12,842 − 9,685 = ____________

10. 8,000 × 50 = ____________

11. 11,943 + 7,880 = ____________

12. 5,116 × 52 = ____________

Solve each problem.

13. An orange grove has 600 orange trees. Each tree produces approximately 300 oranges. How many oranges does the orange grove produce?

____

14. Suppose that last year each tree produced only 270 oranges. How many fewer oranges did the orange grove produce last year?

____

15. A farmer shipped 385 sacks of oranges in 2 trucks, with 125 oranges in a sack. If one truck carries 206 *sacks,* how many *oranges* will the other truck carry?

____

NAME

SHARPEN YOUR SKILLS

Make a Table

1. Shelly left home at 2 P.M. to go for a long walk. She walked at about 10 blocks per half hour. Complete the middle column in the table to show how far Shelly was from home at each time.

2. Shelly's brother Pat left at 2:30 on his bicycle to catch up with Shelly. He rode at a speed of 15 blocks per half hour. Complete the right column to show where Pat was at each given time.

Time	Blocks from Home Shelly	Pat
2:00		
2:30		
3:00		
3:30		
4:00		

3. At what time did Pat catch up with Shelly?

____

Knowing that Maytown is 200 miles from Dango by bus, train, or car, make a table to solve each problem. **Remember** to label your table accurately.

4. Joanne left Dango at 6 A.M., driving at an average speed of 30 miles per hour. Julio left an hour later, driving at 50 miles per hour. How far from Dango were they when Julio caught up with Joanne?

____

5. A train left Dango for Maytown at noon and averaged 80 miles per hour. A bus from Dango, averaging 50 miles per hour, arrived in Maytown at the same time as the train. What time did the bus leave Maytown?

____

6. When the bus left Dango for Maytown at 6 A.M., another bus left Maytown for Dango. If both buses averaged 25 miles per hour, at what time did they meet?

____

7. Lisa can rent a car for $35 a day plus 10¢ a mile or for $40 per day with no mileage fee. How many miles must she drive to make the $40-a-day car more worthwhile?

____

NAME

SHARPEN YOUR SKILLS

Multiplying Decimals

Multiply.

1. 13.6×8

2. 1.36×8

3. 1.36×0.8

4. 0.136×0.8

5. 8.7×0.6

6. 4.70×0.28

7. 40.7×0.3

8. 6.52×9.8

9. 10.02×1.6

10. $0.6 \times 7.3 =$ ______

11. $0.03 \times 29.1 =$ ______

12. $4.2 \times 51.3 =$ ______

13. $0.316 \times 2.53 =$ ______

14. $20 \times 0.9 =$ ______

15. $0.85 \times 18.5 =$ ______

16. $1.365 \times 10 =$ ______

17. $12.4 \times 1.821 =$ ______

Mixed Practice For Exercises 18–23, tell whether you would use paper and pencil, mental math, or a calculator. Then find each product.

18. $1.14 \times 0.87 =$ ______

19. $9.5 \times 10 =$ ______

20. $3.4 \times 200 =$ ______

21. $346 \times 27 =$ ______

22. $6.5 \times 6.2 =$ ______

23. $6.5 \times 600 =$ ______

Critical Thinking Look at Exercises 10–17. Which of these have products greater than the product in Exercise 3?

______

NAME

SHARPEN YOUR SKILLS

Multiplying Decimals: Zeros in the Product

Multiply.

1. $\begin{array}{r} 0.01 \\ \times\ 5.1 \\ \hline \end{array}$

2. $\begin{array}{r} 0.41 \\ \times 0.06 \\ \hline \end{array}$

3. $\begin{array}{r} 0.076 \\ \times\ 1.06 \\ \hline \end{array}$

4. $\begin{array}{r} 0.005 \\ \times\ 2.6 \\ \hline \end{array}$

5. $\begin{array}{r} 0.03 \\ \times\ 1.1 \\ \hline \end{array}$

6. $\begin{array}{r} 0.089 \\ \times\ 3.6 \\ \hline \end{array}$

7. $0.5 \times 2.5 \times 0.04 =$ ________

8. $1.4 \times 0.07 \times 0.08 =$ ________

9. $0.1 \times 1.1 \times 0.11 =$ ________

10. $0.6 \times 0.32 \times 0.2 =$ ________

11. $7.4 \times 1.9 \times 0.03 =$ ________

12. $0.08 \times 1.8 \times 0.1 =$ ________

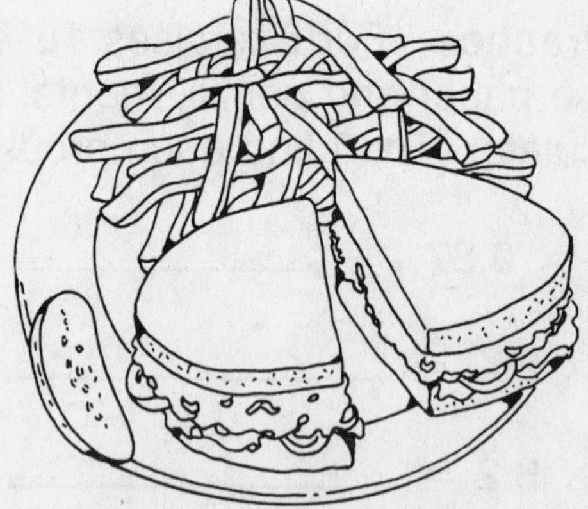

Solve each problem.

13. The cost of a fish sandwich is $1.02. Find the total cost for 3 sandwiches.

____

14. On a class trip, 30 students had a fish sandwich. Use mental math to find the total cost of 30 sandwiches.

____

15. With tomatoes and onions, the sandwich costs $0.25 more. How much do 30 sandwiches at this price cost?

____

NAME

SHARPEN YOUR SKILLS

Mental Math: Multiplying Decimals by Powers of 10

Multiply. Use mental math.

1. $\begin{array}{r} 0.0147 \\ \times \quad 10 \\ \hline \end{array}$

2. $\begin{array}{r} 0.631 \\ \times \quad 100 \\ \hline \end{array}$

3. $\begin{array}{r} 13.109 \\ \times \quad 100 \\ \hline \end{array}$

4. $\begin{array}{r} 0.7305 \\ \times \quad 1{,}000 \\ \hline \end{array}$

5. $\begin{array}{r} 0.69346 \\ \times \quad 10{,}000 \\ \hline \end{array}$

6. $\begin{array}{r} 38.7211 \\ \times \quad 10{,}000 \\ \hline \end{array}$

7. 80.57 × 100 = ____________

8. 0.00615 × 1,000 = ____________

9. 0.08903 × 10,000 = ____________

10. 3.014 × 10,000 = ____________

Complete this table.

Item	Unit Price	Price per 10	Price per 100	Price per 1,000
Juice	$0.57/can	**11.**	**12.**	**13.**
Rye Bread	$1.06 /loaf	**14.**	**15.**	**16.**
Cheese	$3.38 /lb	**17.**	**18.**	**19.**
Turkey	**20.** /whole	**21.**	$2,250	**22.**

NAME

SHARPEN YOUR SKILLS

Deciding When an Estimate Is Enough

Decide whether an estimate is sufficient to answer the question. Explain why. If an exact answer is needed, find the answer.

1. The Pep Club wants to buy T-shirts for each of the 18 members. The shirts cost $8.00 each. Can the club buy the shirts for $150.00?

2. The club will charge $4.25 per car and wash 10 cars every hour. Will they earn at least $75.00 if they work 2 hours?

3. The club sells booster buttons. It costs the club $2.98 for each button. If they have $63.00, can they buy 20 buttons?

4. The club members plan to sell 20 booster buttons. If they sell each button for $3.50, will they receive at least $60.00?

5. There is $29.68 in the club treasury to spend on supplies. Can the members purchase paper for $9.21, paint for $7.64, and pens for $5.85?

6. The club members voted to spend $20.00 for pompons. If each pompon costs $1.25, can they buy one for each of the 18 members?

NAME

SHARPEN YOUR SKILLS

Dividing to Find Missing Factors

Look at Exercises 1–9. Which of these can you do mentally? Solve each equation for *n*. **Remember** to get the unknown number by itself.

1. $3 \times n = 150$

$n =$ ________

2. $5 \times n = 210$

$n =$ ________

3. $n \times 7 = 574$

$n =$ ________

4. $n \times 6 = 4{,}446$

$n =$ ________

5. $n \times 9 = 5{,}886$

$n =$ ________

6. $3 \times n = 2{,}946$

$n =$ ________

7. $n \times 42 = 6{,}552$

$n =$ ________

8. $23 \times n = 2{,}047$

$n =$ ________

9. $n \times 15 = 1{,}110$

$n =$ ________

Complete each diagram.

10.

5	×		=	40
×		×		×
	×	15	=	
=		=		=
60	×		=	7,200

11.

	×	12	=	
×		×		×
18	×		=	54
=		=		=
	×	36	=	7,776

NAME

SHARPEN YOUR SKILLS

Mental Math: Division

Find each quotient mentally.

1. 42 ÷ 6 ______

2. 420 ÷ 6 ______

3. 4,200 ÷ 6 ______

4. 4,200 ÷ 60 ______

Mixed Practice Help the cat find the mouse. Find each answer mentally. Then follow the answers in order.

5. 4 × 5 ______

6. 7 × 100 ______

7. 55 ÷ 5 ______

8. 15 × 0 ______

9. 110 ÷ 5 ______

10. 70 ÷ 7 ______

11. 12 × 10 ______

12. 14 × 1,000 ______

13. 36 ÷ 6 ______

14. 7 × 9,000 ______

15. 150 ÷ 3 ______

16. 5 × 600 ______

START

20	700	43	12	36
99	11	56	6	63,000
5	0	66	14,000	50
21	22	10	120	3,000

END

NAME

SHARPEN YOUR SKILLS

Estimating Quotients

Estimate each quotient by using compatible numbers.

1. 430 ÷ 7 ______

2. 365 ÷ 4 ______

3. 1,256 ÷ 12 ______

4. 599 ÷ 5 ______

5. 619 ÷ 31 ______

6. 4,332 ÷ 60 ______

7. 792 ÷ 43 ______

8. 203 ÷ 11 ______

Estimate each quotient by finding a range.

9. 565 ÷ 8 ______

10. 748 ÷ 9 ______

11. 301 ÷ 4 ______

12. 157 ÷ 20 ______

13. 215 ÷ 7 ______

14. 2,563 ÷ 50 ______

15. 298 ÷ 10 ______

16. 1,676 ÷ 8 ______

Solve.

17. About how many hours are in 3,678 minutes?

______

18. About how many minutes are in 417 seconds?

______

Critical Thinking About how many hours are in 7,201 seconds?

______

NAME

SHARPEN YOUR SKILLS

One-Digit Divisors

Divide. Show remainders as whole numbers.

1. $8\overline{)96}$ **2.** $6\overline{)91}$ **3.** $7\overline{)526}$ **4.** $6\overline{)428}$

5. $8\overline{)927}$ **6.** $2\overline{)329}$ **7.** $6\overline{)835}$ **8.** $3\overline{)517}$

Divide. Show remainders as fractions.

9. $8\overline{)9{,}929}$ **10.** $4\overline{)9{,}387}$ **11.** $5\overline{)7{,}679}$

12. $4\overline{)4{,}857}$ **13.** $7\overline{)9{,}056}$ **14.** $5\overline{)6{,}866}$

Solve the problem.

15. A yearbook contained 108 pictures. If each page had 9 pictures on it, how many pages were in the yearbook?

____

NAME

SHARPEN YOUR SKILLS

One-Digit Divisors: Zeros in the Quotient

Estimate and then divide. **Remember** to place zeros in the quotient when needed. Show remainders as whole numbers.

1. 5)154   30 R4

2. 8)326

3. 6)425

4. 2)161

5. 3)314

6. 5)1,402

7. 6)2,461

8. 5)7,025

9. 3)3,609

10. 8)8,724

11. 7)28,743

12. 4)28,244

Solve the problem.

13. Edna bought a television set for a total cost, including tax, of $648. If she takes 6 months to pay for it, how much will her monthly payments be?

____

NAME

SHARPEN YOUR SKILLS

Two-Digit Divisors: One-Digit Quotients

Divide.

1. 37)72 **2.** 42)57 **3.** 26)49

4. 64)425 **5.** 58)300 **6.** 92)814

7. 78)629 **8.** 63)532 **9.** 31)295

10. 379 ÷ 40 = ________ **11.** 107 ÷ 56 = ________

Write M or P for whether you would use mental math or paper and pencil. Then find each quotient.

12. 60)480 **13.** 34)329 **14.** 32)68 **15.** 45)90

________ ________ ________ ________

________ ________ ________ ________

NAME

SHARPEN YOUR SKILLS

Interpret the Remainders

Solve each problem.

1. Murphy school is opening in the fall. 400 desks were ordered for 15 classrooms. If each classroom receives the same number of desks, how many desks will be left over?

2. Each school bus can carry 42 students. How many buses will be needed to carry 310 students?

3. There are 3,598 books for the library. Approximately 24 books fit on a shelf. How many shelves are needed?

4. There are 80 chairs in the library. How many tables are needed if only 6 chairs can fit at each table?

5. There are 500 seats in the auditorium. Each row except the last has 36 seats. How many seats are in the last row?

6. How many classrooms will receive 35 rulers if 384 rulers are ordered?

7. If 100 packages of paper are shared equally by 6 teachers, how many packages will be left over?

8. Pencils come 48 in a box. How many boxes should be ordered if 600 pencils are needed?

Use after pages 106–107.

NAME

SHARPEN YOUR SKILLS

Adjusting Quotients

Estimate and then divide. Write each remainder as a whole number.

1. 72)207 ______

2. 48)293 ______

3. 16)92 ______

4. 55)432 ______

5. 22)215 ______

6. 76)587 ______

7. 35)289 ______

8. 68)399 ______

9. 69)200 ______

10. 18)119 ______

11. 52)402 ______

12. 36)167 ______

13. 43)289 ______

14. 64)560 ______

15. 45)245 ______

16. 19)183 ______

Mixed Practice Find each answer.

Remember to watch the signs.

17. 34 × 102 ______

18. 97 + 345 ______

19. 20)180 ______

20. 4,567 − 2,989 ______

21. 2,453 + 432 ______

22. 44)352 ______

23. 14)73 ______

24. 4,765 × 56 ______

NAME

SHARPEN YOUR SKILLS

Two-Digit Divisors: Two or More Digits in the Quotient

Fill in the first two columns of Exercises 1–4 by using the numbers in the figure at the right. Then divide. Write each remainder as a whole number.

An example is given.

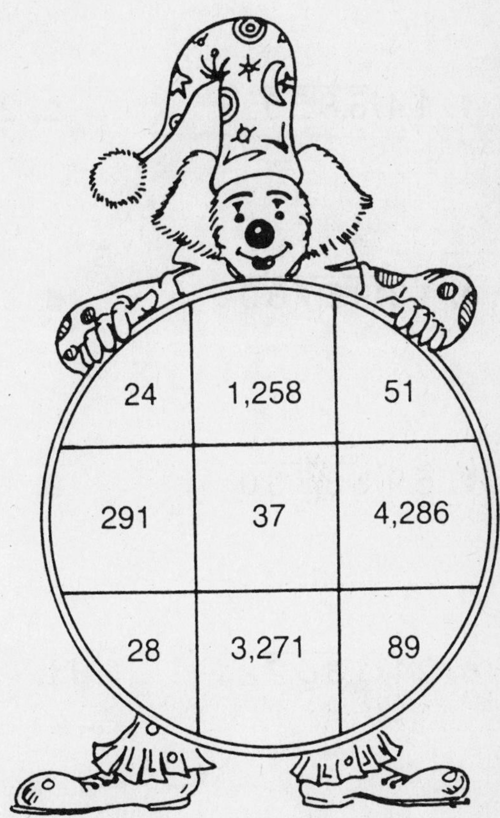

1. 1,258 ÷ 24 = 52 R10

2. ______ ÷ ______ = ______

3. ______ ÷ ______ ______

4.

Divide. Write each remainder as a whole number.

5. $51\overline{)7,428}$

6. $74\overline{)7,342}$

7. $85\overline{)9,475}$

8. $20\overline{)3,755}$

9. $43\overline{)5,889}$

10. $38\overline{)6,635}$

11. $47\overline{)6,186}$

12. $18\overline{)7,763}$

13. $63\overline{)34,218}$

NAME

SHARPEN YOUR SKILLS

Two-Digit Divisors: Zeros in the Quotient

What is the tallest mountain in the continental United States?

To find out, divide. Then write each letter above its matching answer below. Two answers are not used.

1. 14)8,820 **T**

2. 22)8,888 **H**

3. 38)73,080 **I**

4. 13)95,760 **B**

5. 33)65,224 **•**

6. 25)75,300 **A**

7. 69)58,890 **N**

8. 14)6,024 **W**

9. 37)11,433 **T**

10. 21)130,221 **E**

11. 47)49,961 **M**

12. 47)43,200 **Y**

____	____	____
1063	**630**	**1,976 R16**

____	____	____	____	____	____	____
430 R4	**404**	**1,923 R6**	**309**	**853 R33**	**6,201**	**919 R7**

Mental Math Try to use mental math to divide.

13. 33)6,600 ____

14. 40)3,600 ____

15. 15)9,000 ____

16. 80)2,407 ____

17. 5,200 ÷ 13 ____

18. 450,000 ÷ 90 ____

19. 2,703 ÷ 30 ____

20. 8,105 ÷ 90 ____

NAME

SHARPEN YOUR SKILLS

Write an Equation

Write an equation. Then solve the problem.

1. A family traveled 1,840 miles by train and by car on a vacation trip. If the family traveled 430 miles by train, how many miles did the family travel by car?

____

____

2. The family spent $40 for souvenirs and $120 for gasoline on their trip. The amount spent for gasoline is how many times the amount spent for souvenirs?

____

____

3. The cost of the guided tour was $12 per person. How many members of the family went if the amount spent on the tour was $48?

____

____

4. The amount spent on lodging was $320 for 8 days. What was the average amount spent on lodging per day?

____

____

5. The family drove 620 miles in one day. In the morning, they drove 239 miles. How many miles did they drive in the afternoon?

____

____

6. The amount spent on the vacation trip was about $2,560. Last year $1,740 was spent on the vacation trip. What was the difference on the amount spent?

____

____

NAME

SHARPEN YOUR SKILLS

Estimating Quotients

Without dividing, write whether the quotient is greater than or less than 1.

1. 3.5 ÷ 1 ______

2. 83.6 ÷ 13 ______

3. 30.3 ÷ 14 ______

4. $234\overline{)1890}$ ______

5. $38\overline{)12.7}$ ______

6. $5\overline{)4.5}$ ______

7. $15\overline{)71.9}$ ______

8. $56\overline{)57.2}$ ______

9. $15\overline{)13.5}$ ______

Find a range to estimate the quotient.

10. 63 ÷ 8 ______

11. 148.4 ÷ 25 ______

12. 45.3 ÷ 9 ______

13. $35\overline{)99}$ ______

14. $7\overline{)703}$ ______

15. $4\overline{)38}$ ______

16. $25\overline{)209.7}$ ______

17. $10\overline{)928.67}$ ______

18. $5\overline{)37.68}$ ______

19. $6\overline{)430}$ ______

20. $11\overline{)92.4}$ ______

21. $20\overline{)601.5}$ ______

NAME

SHARPEN YOUR SKILLS

Dividing a Decimal by a Whole Number

Divide. **Remember** to place the decimal point in the quotient.

1. $6\overline{)4.2}$

2. $4\overline{)65.2}$

3. $8\overline{)9.36}$

4. $27\overline{)16.2}$

5. $33\overline{)41.58}$

6. $14\overline{)53.2}$

7. $4\overline{)69.32}$

8. $8\overline{)103.2}$

9. $15\overline{)604.05}$

10. $16\overline{)2{,}232.32}$

11. $7\overline{)157.15}$

12. $14\overline{)785.4}$

13. $7\overline{)60.48}$

14. $6\overline{)1.956}$

15. $15\overline{)278.40}$

Solve the problem.

16. If 5 cm^3 of gold has a weight of 96.5 g, what is the density of gold in grams per cubic centimeter?

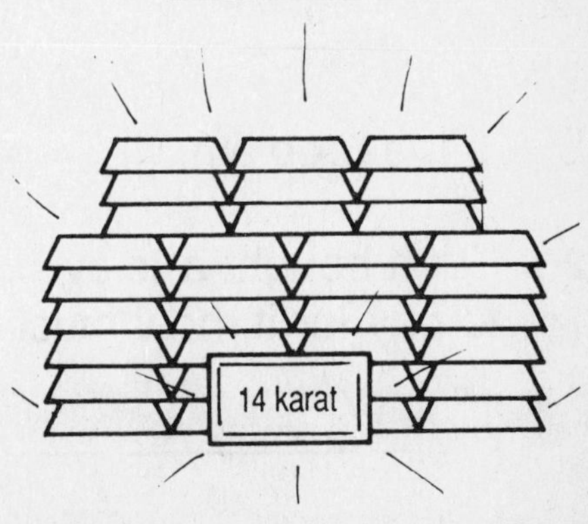

SHARPEN YOUR SKILLS

Writing Zeros in the Quotient

Find each quotient.

1. $5\overline{)3.5}$ _____
2. $80\overline{)64.2}$ _____
3. $36\overline{)18.9}$ _____
4. $3\overline{).009}$ _____
5. $23\overline{)13.8}$ _____
6. $7\overline{)6.3}$ _____
7. $12\overline{)9.6}$ _____
8. $15\overline{)7.5}$ _____
9. $5\overline{)15.4}$ _____
10. $8\overline{)32.6}$ _____
11. $6\overline{)42.3}$ _____
12. $2\overline{)16.1}$ _____
13. $3\overline{)31.5}$ _____
14. $5\overline{)1.402}$ _____
15. $7\overline{)21.63}$ _____
16. $4\overline{)2.432}$ _____
17. $24.63 \div 6 =$ _____
18. $70.25 \div 5 =$ _____
19. $36.09 \div 3 =$ _____
20. $872.4 \div 8 =$ _____
21. $28.743 \div 7 =$ _____
22. $28.244 \div 4 =$ _____

Solve the problem.

23. Edna bought a television set for $648.00. If she takes 6 months to pay for it, how much will her monthly payments be?

_____

Use after pages 134–135.

NAME ______

Mental Math: Dividing by 10, 100, 1,000

Use mental math to divide by moving the decimal point.

Remember to count the zeros in the divisor.

1. 50.4 ÷ 10 ______

2. 5,987 ÷ 100 ______

3. 730.7 ÷ 1000 ______

4. 98.6 ÷ 100 ______

5. 56,702 ÷ 100 ______

6. 89.42 ÷ 10 ______

7. 0.0342 ÷ 100 ______

8. 4.309 ÷ 1000 ______

9. 478 ÷ 100 ______

10. 22.22 ÷ 100 ______

11. 14.467 ÷ 10 ______

12. 328.4 ÷ 1000 ______

Solve each problem.

A survey found that in a certain town there were 35 cats per 100 people and 29 dogs per 100 people.

13. How many cats per person were there? ______

14. How many dogs per person were there? ______

Critical Thinking What do you think it means to have 0.35 cats per person?

______

______

SHARPEN YOUR SKILLS

Expressing Fractions as Decimals

Write each fraction as a decimal.

Remember to divide the numerator by the denominator.

1. $\frac{3}{8}$ ______ **2.** $\frac{1}{5}$ ______ **3.** $\frac{5}{8}$ ______ **4.** $\frac{4}{5}$ ______ **5.** $\frac{12}{32}$ ______

6. $\frac{12}{25}$ ______ **7.** $\frac{5}{16}$ ______ **8.** $\frac{9}{10}$ ______ **9.** $\frac{7}{16}$ ______ **10.** $\frac{3}{4}$ ______

Use your calculator or pencil and paper to write these fractions as decimals rounded to the nearest hundredth.

11. $\frac{4}{15}$ ______ **12.** $\frac{3}{7}$ ______ **13.** $\frac{5}{9}$ ______ **14.** $\frac{6}{7}$ ______ **15.** $\frac{1}{32}$ ______

Critical Thinking Solve each of the following problems.

16. John can high-jump $6\frac{3}{8}$ feet. How does this compare to the class record of 6.9 feet?

______

17. Did he break the class record on his last jump of $6\frac{7}{8}$ feet? Explain.

______

Use after pages 138–139.

NAME ____________________

SHARPEN YOUR SKILLS

Repeating Decimals

Write each fraction as a repeating decimal.

Remember to put a bar over the digit or digits that repeat.

1. $\frac{3}{9}$ ______ **2.** $\frac{1}{11}$ ______ **3.** $\frac{1}{3}$ ______ **4.** $\frac{5}{12}$ ______ **5.** $\frac{2}{3}$ ______

6. $\frac{7}{15}$ ______ **7.** $\frac{5}{9}$ ______ **8.** $\frac{10}{55}$ ______ **9.** $\frac{4}{9}$ ______ **10.** $\frac{10}{99}$ ______

11. $\frac{7}{12}$ ______ **12.** $\frac{17}{24}$ ______ **13.** $\frac{8}{9}$ ______ **14.** $\frac{8}{15}$ ______ **15.** $\frac{6}{11}$ ______

Cross out each box that contains one of the answers above. Write the remaining letters in the blanks below to answer the riddle. Some answers are not used.

What runs but never walks?

B $0.4\overline{6}$	**D** $0.\overline{18}$	**W** 0.79	**L** $0.41\overline{6}$	**S** $0.\overline{6}$	**A** 0.302	**V** $0.\overline{54}$
T 0.577	**P** $0.5\overline{3}$	**G** $0.\overline{09}$	**N** $0.\overline{10}$	**E** 0.7029	**K** $0.708\overline{3}$	**R** 0.7

ANSWER . . . . ____ ____ ____ ____ ____

SHARPEN YOUR SKILLS

Give Sensible Answers

Give each answer.

The Wangs drove across the country on their vacation. They took a month to make the trip.

1. During the first 5 days, they drove 1,589 miles. About how many miles did they drive each day?

____

2. The sixth day, the Wangs drove 469 miles in 9 hours. About how many miles per hour did they average?

____

3. The station wagon gets 38 miles per gallon of gas. About how many gallons of gas did the car use on the sixth day of the trip?

____

4. If gas costs $1.40 per gallon, about how much did they spend on gas on the sixth day?

____

5. About how many gallons of gas did they use during the first five days?

____

6. About how much did they spend on gas during the first five days of the trip?

____

7. On the seventh day, the Wangs drove 152 miles in 6 hours. About how many miles per hour did they average?

____

8. Based on the Wangs mileage during the first 7 days of their trip, approximately how many more days will it take them to complete a total distance of 3,000 miles?

____

NAME

SHARPEN YOUR SKILLS

Dividing by a Decimal

Place the decimal point correctly in each quotient.

1. $\begin{array}{r}14\\ 0.4\overline{)5.6}\end{array}$
2. $\begin{array}{r}14\\ 0.4\overline{)0.56}\end{array}$
3. $\begin{array}{r}14\\ 0.4\overline{)0.056}\end{array}$
4. $\begin{array}{r}35\\ 0.47\overline{)1.645}\end{array}$
5. $\begin{array}{r}43\\ 0.3\overline{)1.29}\end{array}$
6. $\begin{array}{r}123\\ 0.06\overline{)7.38}\end{array}$

What is even more unusual than a counting dog?

To find out, work each exercise. Draw a line to the correct answer. Each line will pass through a letter. Write the letter on the blank next to the answer.

Exercise		Answer	
7. $0.8\overline{)3.2}$	★	★ 0.56	____
8. $0.8\overline{)0.32}$	★	★ 0.23	____
9. $0.8\overline{)0.032}$	★	★ 0.4	____
10. $0.9\overline{)0.63}$	★	★ 7	____
11. $0.08\overline{)0.56}$	★	★ 23	____
12. $0.008\overline{)0.448}$	★	★ 4	____
13. $0.138 \div 0.6$	★	★ 0.07	____
14. $0.238 \div 3.4$	★	★ 2.3	____
15. $12.88 \div 2.3$	★	★ 0.7	____
16. $1.7\overline{)3.91}$	★	★ 0.04	____
17. $2.7\overline{)1.512}$	★	★ 5.6	____
18. $3.4\overline{)78.2}$	★	★ 56	____

C

P

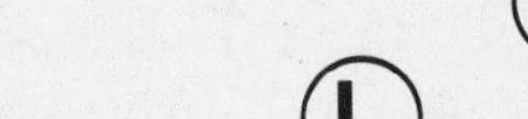

S G L E

A N B E R S

NAME

SHARPEN YOUR SKILLS

Zeros in the Dividend

Divide. **Remember** to add zeros to the dividend as needed.

1. $0.5\overline{)255.}$ **2.** $0.016\overline{)0.8}$ **3.** $4.5\overline{)0.009}$ **4.** $0.045\overline{)90.}$

5. $0.4\overline{)85}$ **6.** $0.6\overline{)261}$ **7.** $0.8\overline{)476}$ **8.** $0.24\overline{)11.7}$

9. $0.48\overline{)16.8}$ **10.** $3.5\overline{)119}$ **11.** $0.72\overline{)3.6}$ **12.** $0.25\overline{)6}$

13. $0.2\overline{)9.5}$ **14.** $0.91\overline{)0.2366}$ **15.** $5.1\overline{)16.32}$ **16.** $0.46\overline{)8.28}$

17. $0.14\overline{)11.9}$ **18.** $0.025\overline{)0.16}$ **19.** $0.3\overline{)28.53}$ **20.** $0.002\overline{)0.06}$

Use after pages 148–149.

NAME

SHARPEN YOUR SKILLS

Choose an Operation

Write what operation you would use to solve each problem. Then give the answer.

1. Leon earned $4.80 each week last summer babysitting a neighbor's children. How much money did he earn in 12 weeks?

____

____

2. Last summer Leon mowed lawns in his neighborhood. He charged $12.50 per lawn and earned $562.50 during the summer. How many lawns did he mow?

____

____

3. Leon deposited the money he earned from babysitting and mowing lawns in his savings account. If this is the only money he deposited, how much did he save last summer?

____

____

4. Priscilla makes yarn cat toys and sells them to a pet store for $2.75 each. The toys cost her $0.28 to make. How much money does she earn on each toy sold?

____

____

5. Priscilla spent $4.20 at the craft store for all the supplies she needs to make the cat toys. How many toys can she make if the cost per toy is $0.28?

____

____

6. The pet store asked Priscilla to make 35 more toys for them to sell. They paid her $2.75 per toy. How much money did Priscilla receive from the pet shop owners?

____

____

SHARPEN YOUR SKILLS

Basic Geometric Ideas

Use the diagram at the right.

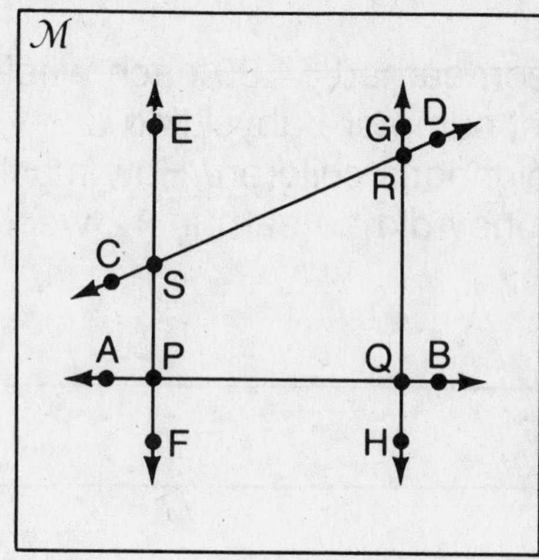

1. Which lines intersect at point R?

____

2. Name two points that are not on $\overleftrightarrow{GH}$.

____

3. Name two points on $\overleftrightarrow{AB}$.

____

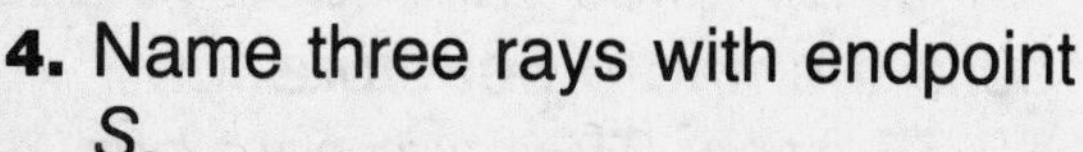

4. Name three rays with endpoint S.

____

5. Which lines intersect $\overleftrightarrow{EF}$?

____

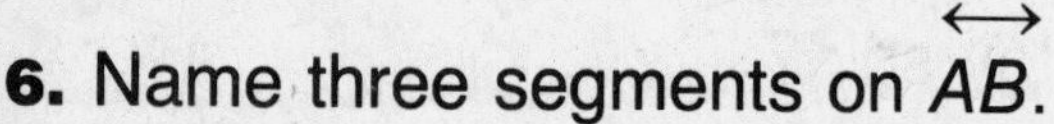

6. Name three segments on $\overleftrightarrow{AB}$.

____

7. What is the endpoint of $\overrightarrow{RD}$?

____

Use the diagram at the right.

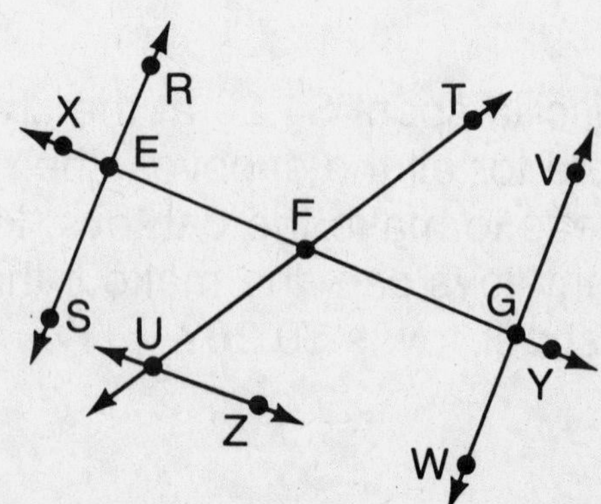

8. Name three rays on $\overleftrightarrow{XY}$.

____

9. Name the intersection of $\overleftrightarrow{XY}$ and $\overleftrightarrow{VW}$.

____

10. Give another name for $\overline{RS}$.

____

NAME

SHARPEN YOUR SKILLS

Angles and Angle Measurement

Name each angle, side, and vertex.

1.

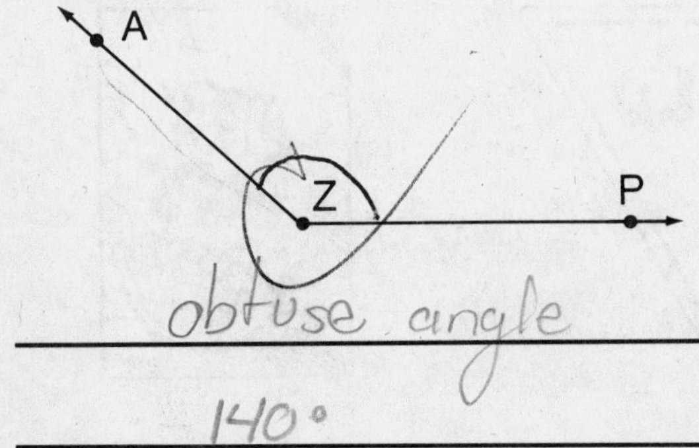

2.

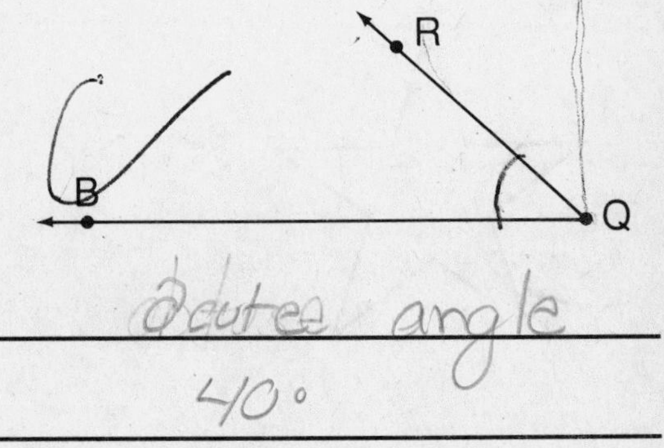

Measure each angle. Then tell whether it is acute, right, or obtuse.

3.

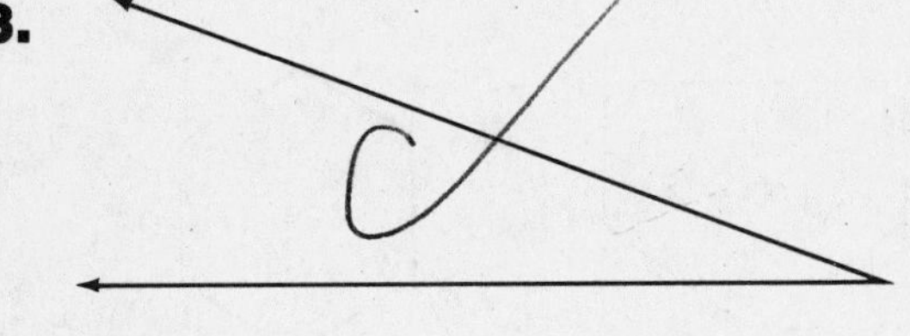

4.

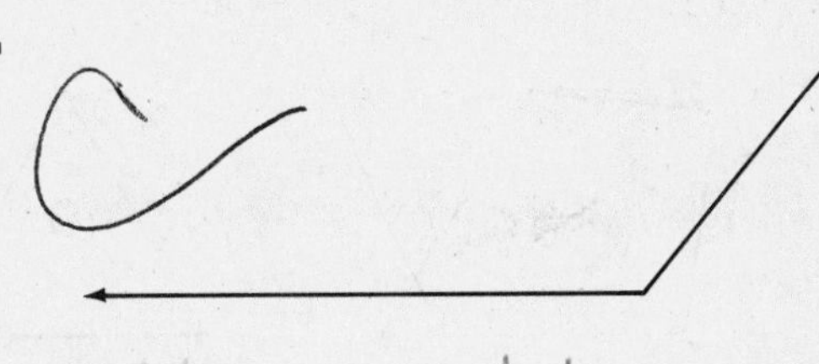

5.

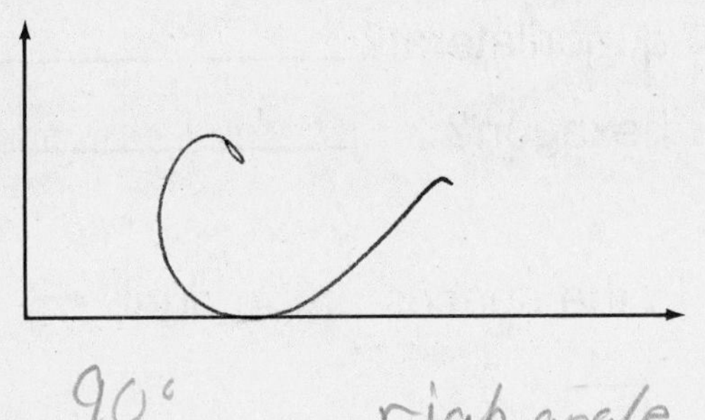

6.

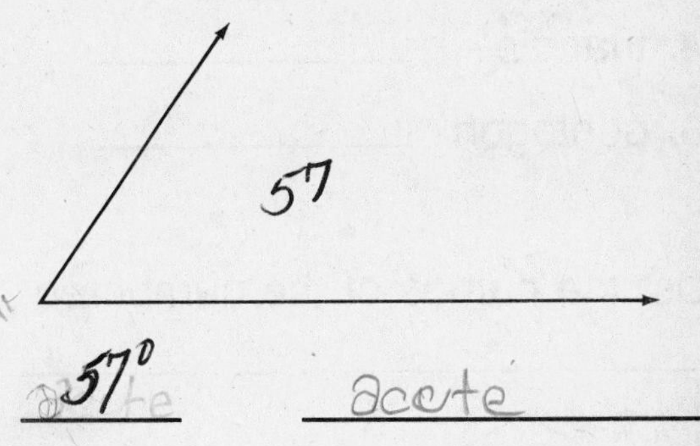

Draw an angle with the given measure.

7. 27°

8. 136°

NAME

SHARPEN YOUR SKILLS

Polygons

Name each polygon.

1. 

______

2. 

______

3. 

______

Use these figures for Exercises 4–7.

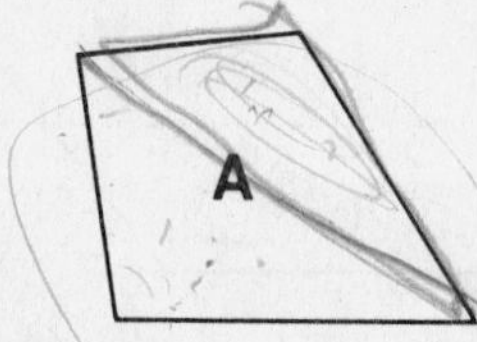

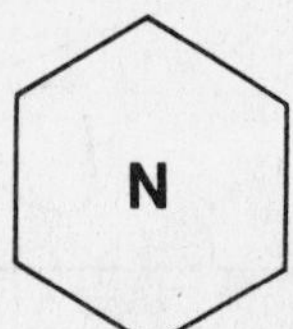

Which figure is a

4. triangle? ______

5. quadrilateral? ______

6. pentagon? ______

7. hexagon? ______

List the names of the numbered polygons in the spaces at the right.

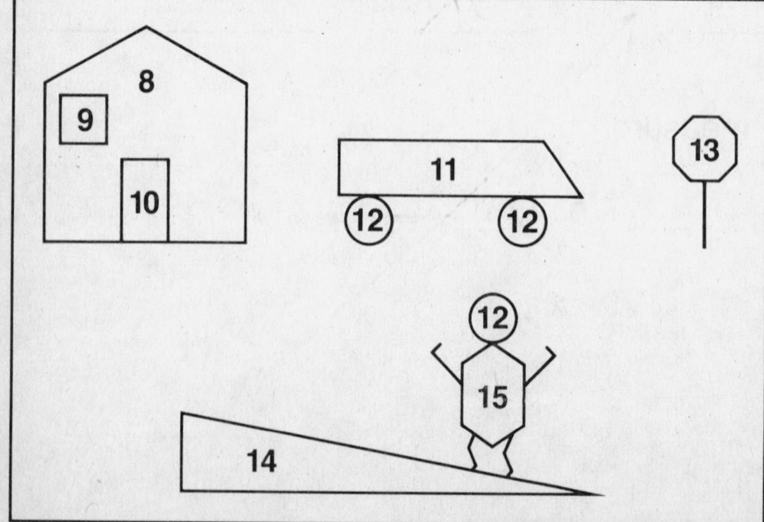

8. ______

9. ______

10. ______

11. ______

12. ______

13. ______

14. ______

15. ______

NAME ____________________

SHARPEN YOUR SKILLS

Types of Triangles

From the pictures shown, identify each triangle as acute, right, or obtuse.

1.

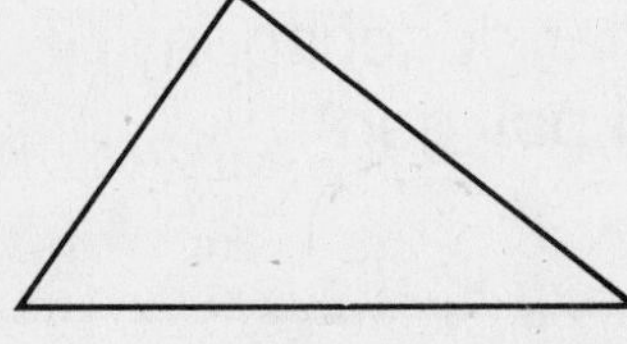

____

2.

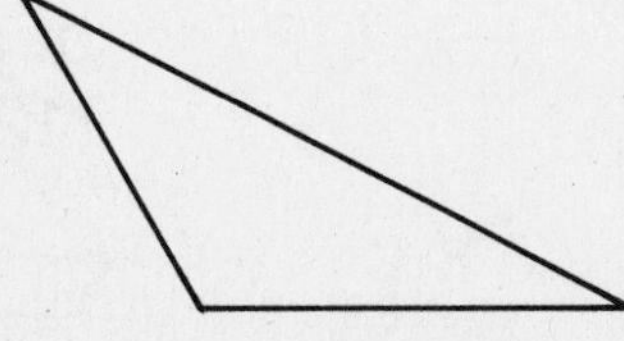

____

3.

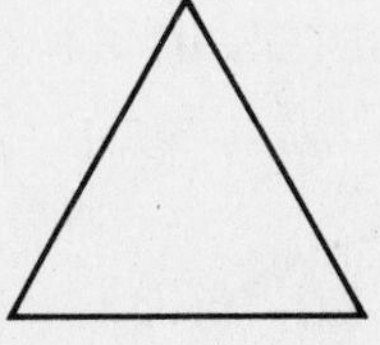

____

4.

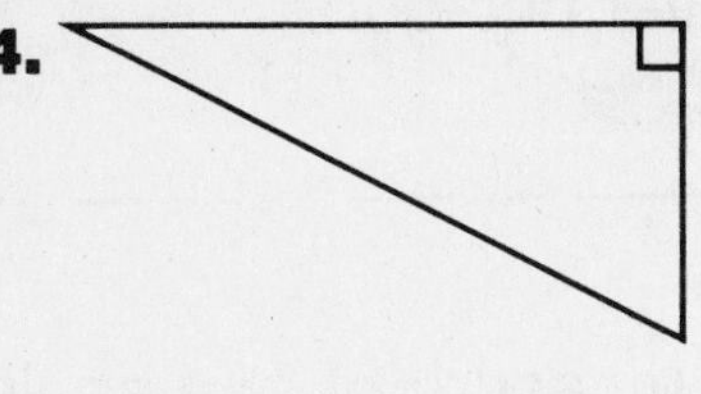

____

5.

____

6.

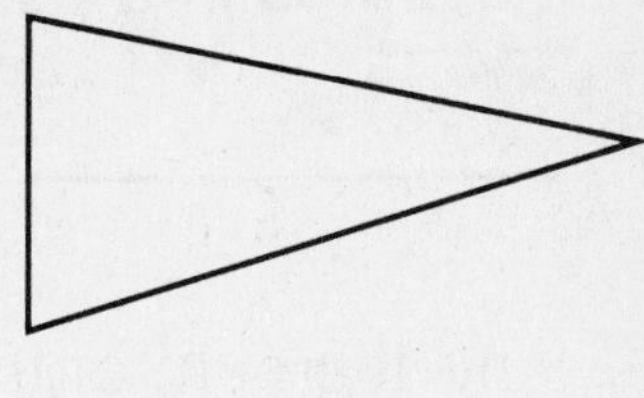

____

Find the third angle measure in each triangle. Identify each triangle as scalene, isosceles, or equilateral.

7.

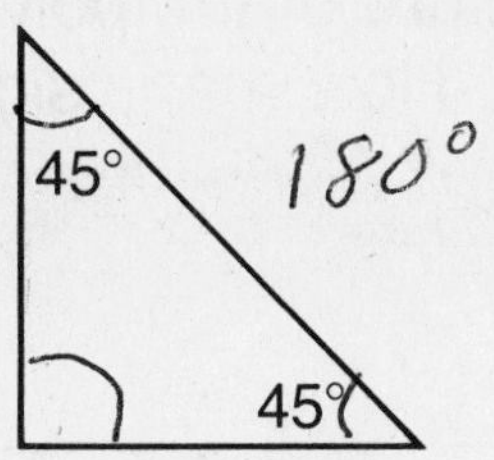

____

____

8.

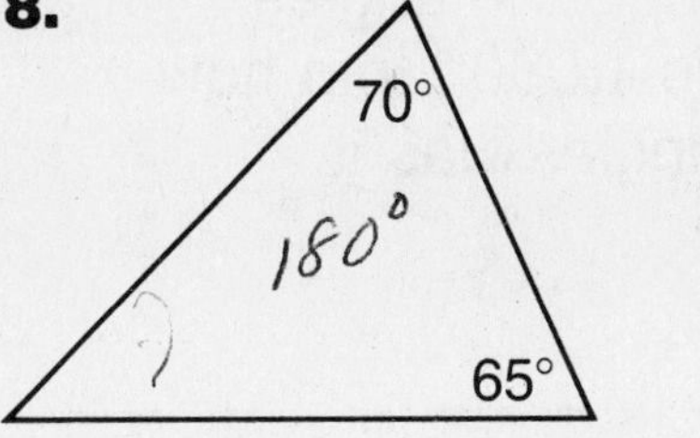

____

____

9.

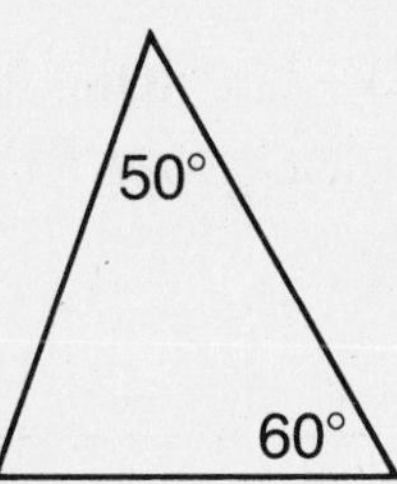

____

____

10.

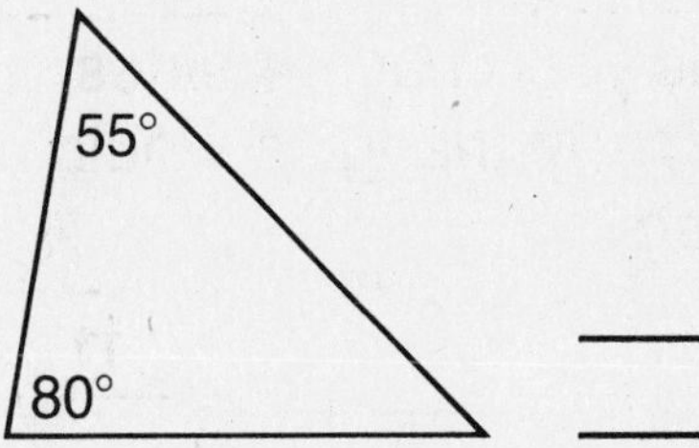

____

____

11.

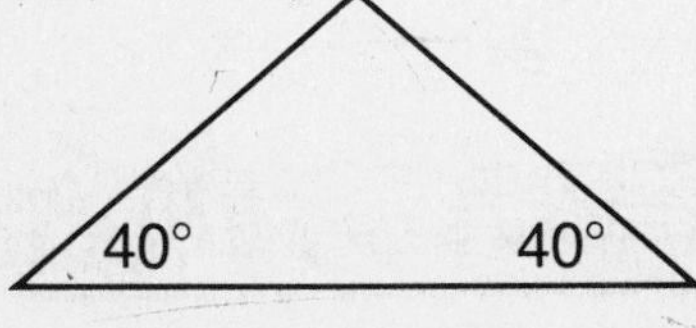

____

____

12.

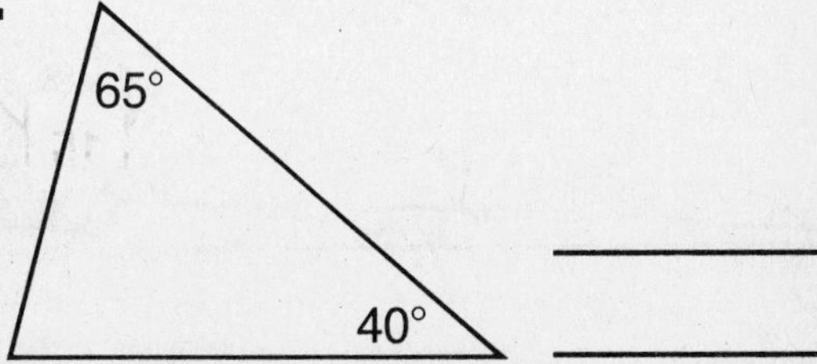

____

____

NAME

SHARPEN YOUR SKILLS

Solve a Simpler Problem

Give each answer.

1. Find the sum of the angle measures in a hexagon.

2. Find the measure of one angle of a regular dodecagon (12-sided polygon).

3. Find the sum of the angle measures in a pentagon.

4. Find the measure of one angle of a regular octagon.

5. Find the sum of the angle measures in a 9-sided polygon.

6. Find the measure of one angle of a regular 9-sided polygon.

7. If the sum of the angles in a polygon is 1,080°, into how many triangles was it divided?

8. Draw a picture of the polygon in Exercise 7. How many sides does it have?

9. If a polygon has 14 sides, into how many triangles would it be divided?

10. What would be the total number of degrees in the polygon in Exercise 9?

NAME

SHARPEN YOUR SKILLS

Quadrilaterals

Give all the names that apply to each figure. Use *trapezoid, parallelogram, rhombus, rectangle,* and *square.*

1. 

2. 

3. 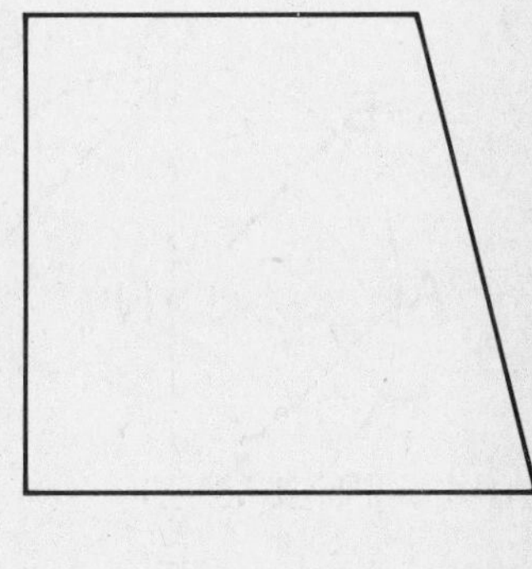

4. 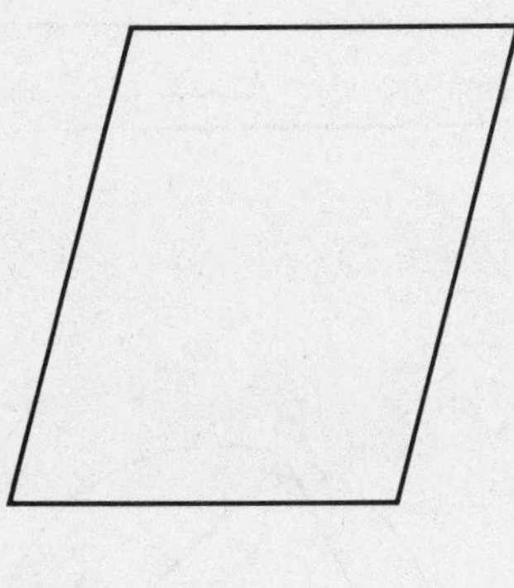

5. 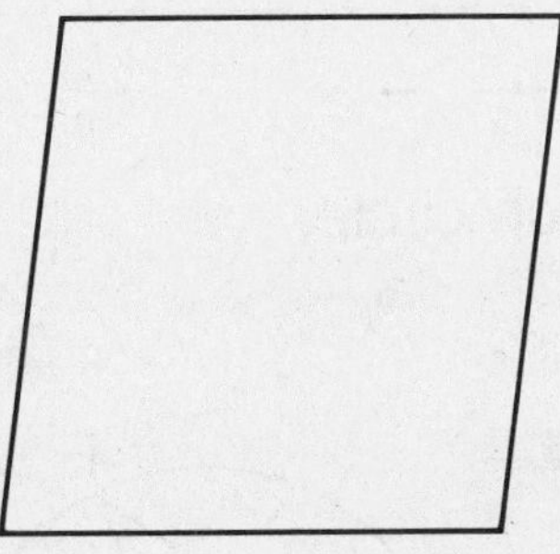

6.

Give each answer.

7. What additional characteristics are needed in a rhombus to make it square?

8. What is the difference between a rhombus and a parallelogram?

SHARPEN YOUR SKILLS

Circles

Name each radius and two chords.
In each circle, point *N* is the center.

1.

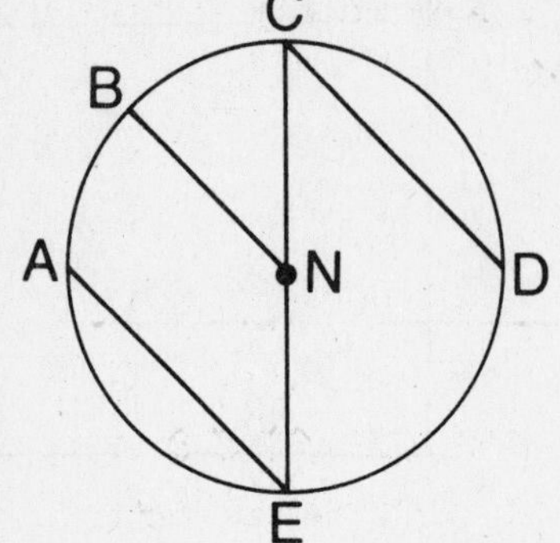

2.

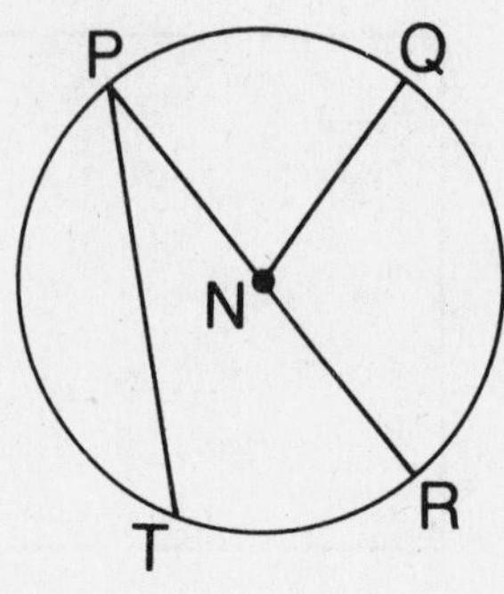

3.

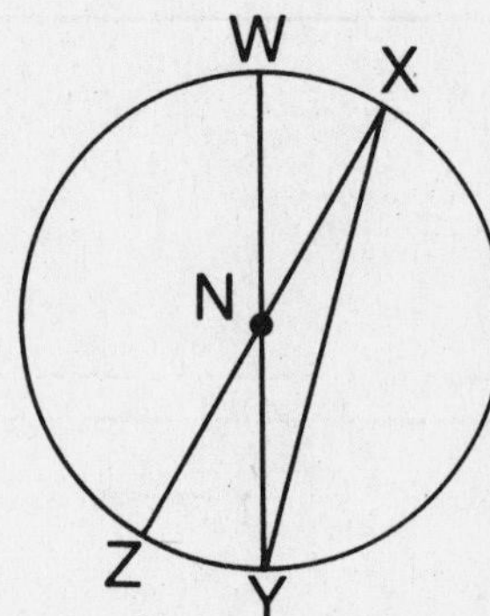

Name each diameter. In each circle, point *S* is the center.

4.

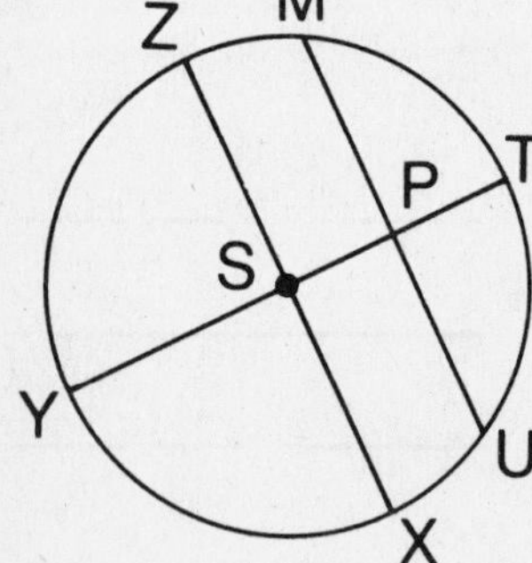

5.

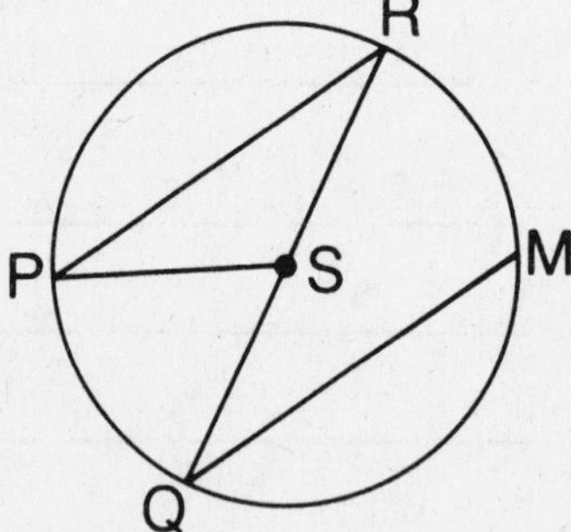

6.

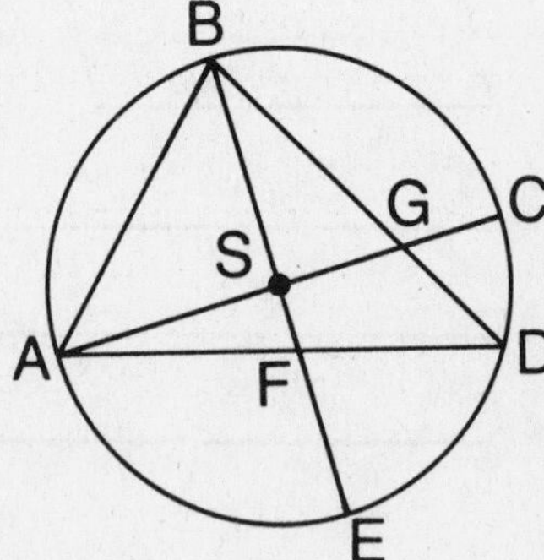

Solve each problem.

7. A disk has a 12-inch diameter. What is the radius?

8. A disk has an $11\frac{1}{2}$-inch radius. What is the diameter?

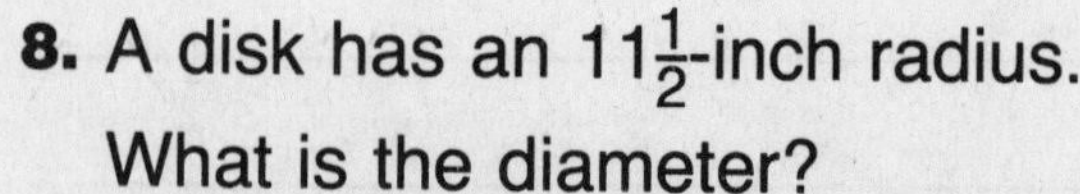

NAME

SHARPEN YOUR SKILLS

Use Logical Reasoning

Solve each problem.

1. Six baseball teams are playing in a tournament. Each team plays each other team one time. How many games will be played?

 ____

2. If two teams are added to the tournament how many games will be played?

 ____

3. All 8 team managers presented each other team with a bat. How many bats were exchanged?

 ____

4. When the manager of the winning team accepted the trophy, the other 7 managers shook hands with every other manager once. How many handshakes took place?

 ____

5. The winning team was so pleased that each of the 15 players shook hands with each other member of the team one time. How many handshakes took place?

 ____

6. If the manager of the winning team joined the handshaking, how many handshakes would take place then?

 ____

SHARPEN YOUR SKILLS

Congruent and Similar Figures

Write if each pair of figures is congruent, similar, or neither.

1.

2.

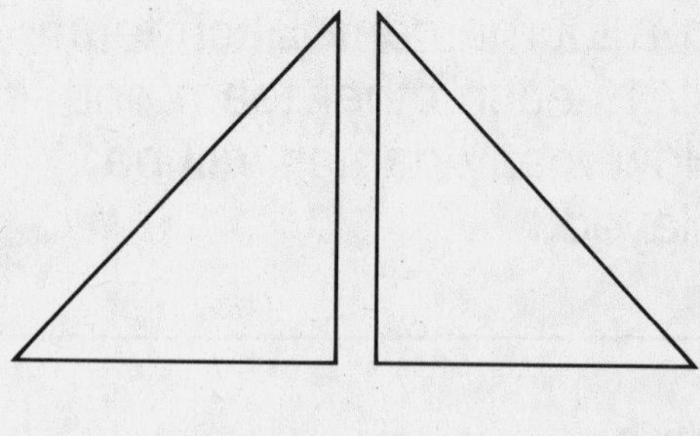

3.

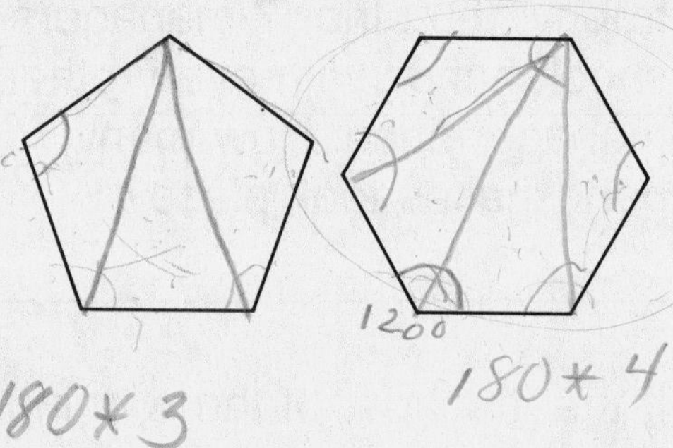

4.

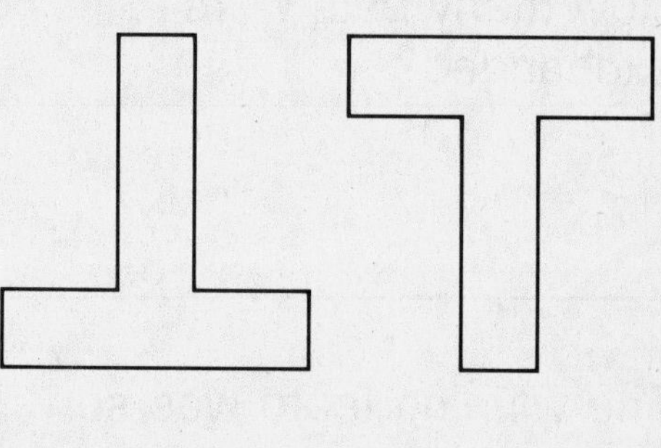

5.

6.

7. Draw a figure that is congruent to the figure below.

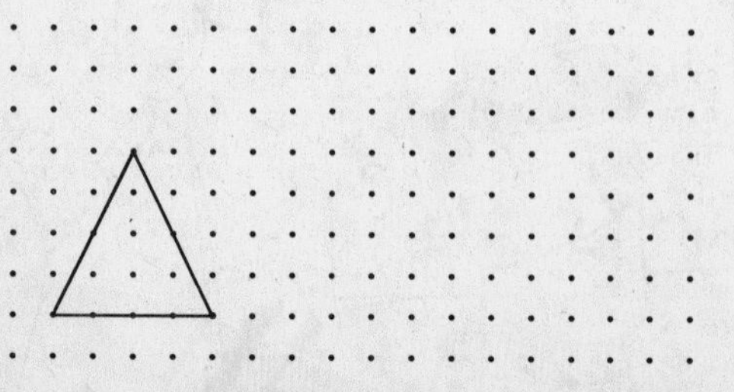

8. Draw a figure that is similar to the figure below.

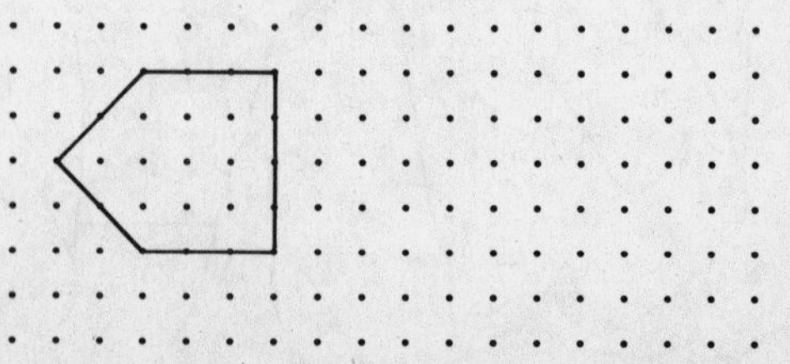

Use after pages 184–185.

NAME

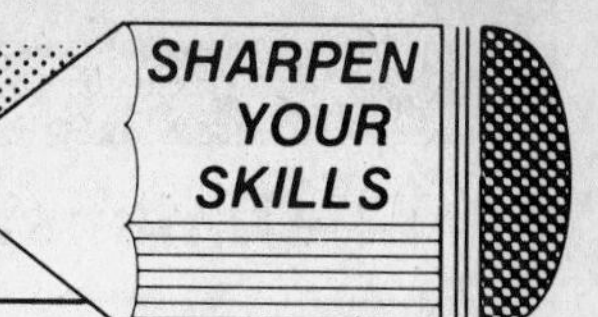

Transformations

Describe how to get from Figure I to Figure II.
Write *slide, flip,* or *turn*.

1.

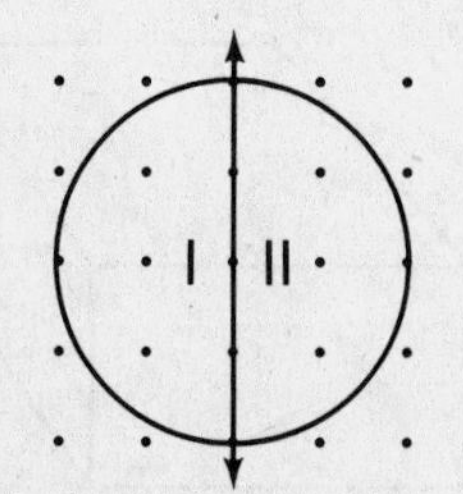

2.

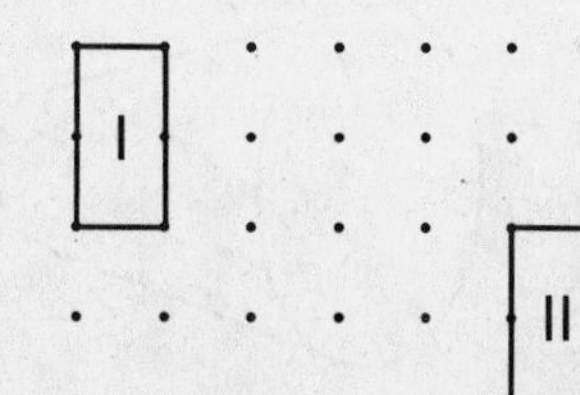

3.

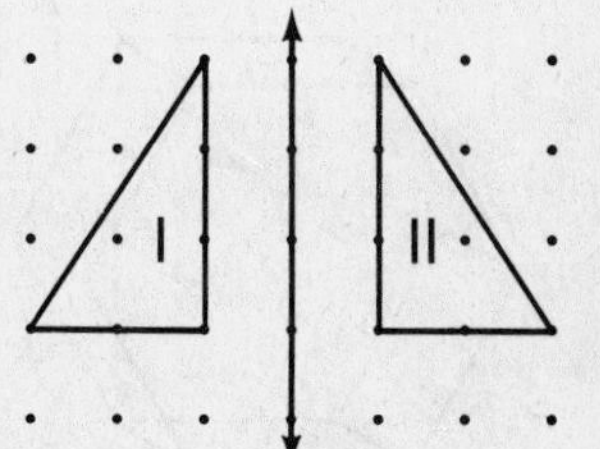

4.

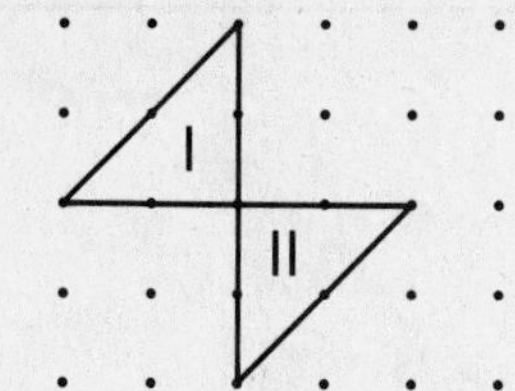

5.

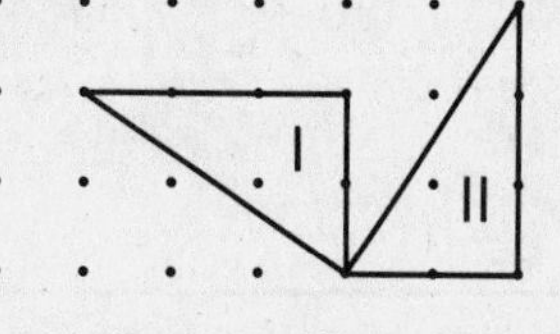

6.

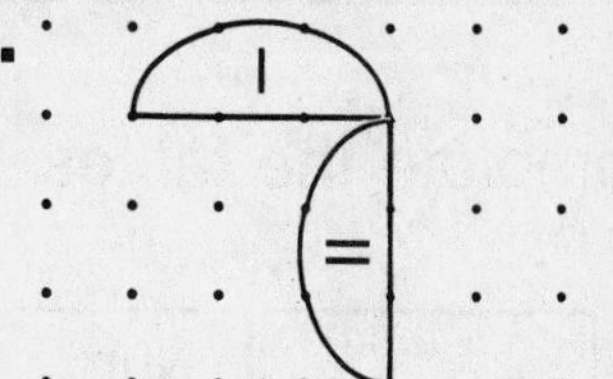

Complete the following.

7. Draw triangle *DEF*. Show a slide 3 units down and 2 units right.

8. Draw rectangle *ABCD*. Show a flip over side *CD*.

9. Draw a triangle *HIJ*. Show a 90° counterclockwise turn about point *I*.

10. Draw square *LMNO*. Show a slide 3 units up.

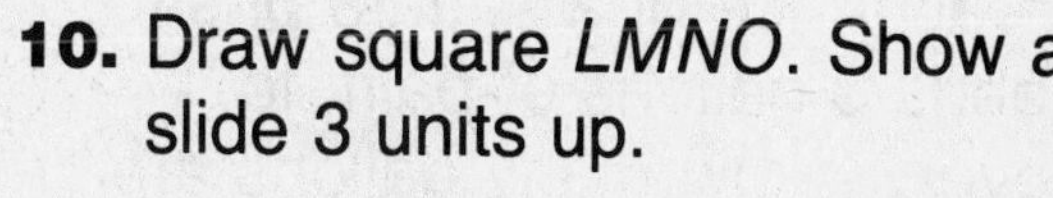

NAME

Three-Dimensional Figures

Tell whether each of the following is a polyhedron. Write *yes* or *no*.

1. 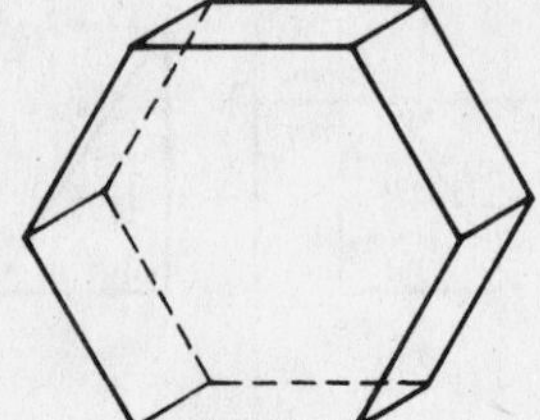

______

2. 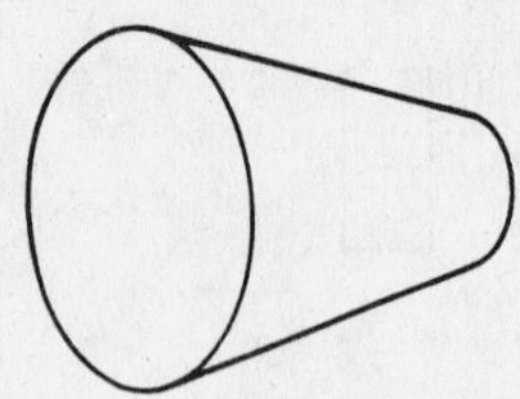

______

3. 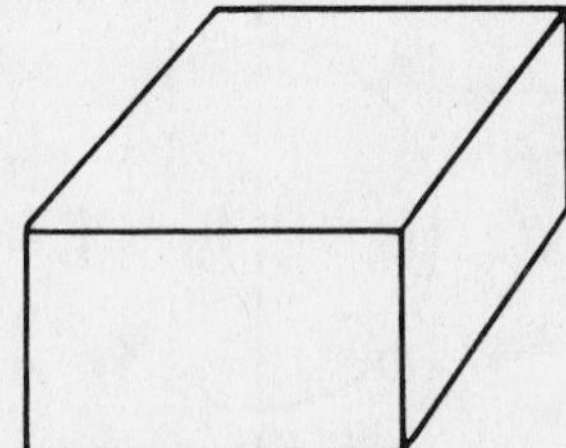

______

Complete the tables.

4.

Pyramid	Number of faces	Number of vertices	Number of edges
3-sided			
7-sided			

5.

Prism	Number of faces	Number of vertices	Number of edges
3-sided			
9-sided			

6. If each face of a square prism needs 3 gallons of paint to cover it, how many gallons are needed to paint the whole cube?

______

7. Each vertex of a hexagonal pyramid needs one dot of yellow paint. How many yellow dots of paint are needed?

______

NAME

SHARPEN YOUR SKILLS

Divisibility Rules

Write *Yes* or *No* in each box of the table to tell if the numbers on the left are divisible by the numbers at the top.

	Number	Divisible by					
		2	3	5	6	10	25
1.	26						
2.	27						
3.	30						
4.	32						
5.	42						
6.	50						

Complete each sentence.

7. For a number to be divisible by 2, the digit in the ones place must be ______________________.

8. For a number to be divisible by 5, the digit in the ones place must be ______________________.

9. For a number to be divisible by 10, the digit in the ones place must be ______________________.

10. For a number to be divisible by 3, the sum of the digits must be ______________________.

NAME

SHARPEN YOUR SKILLS

Prime and Composite Numbers

Tell if the number is prime or composite. Write *P* or *C*.

1. 169 ______ **2.** 113 ______ **3.** 270 ______ **4.** 329 ______

For each number, write the prime factorization using exponents. You may want to use a factor tree.

5. 252 ______ **6.** 72 ______ **7.** 512 ______ **8.** 135 ______

9. 1,250 ______ **10.** 80 ______ **11.** 3,888 ______ **12.** 300 ______

Circle the numbers that are prime. Shade in prime numbers on the picture.

13. 3 6 7 15 21 26

14. 2 4 5 9 13 19

15. 14 17 18 24 29 30

16. 22 23 31 33 35 38

17. 5 11 12 41 49 51

18. 28 37 39 40 45 53

19. 16 25 27 32 47 52

20. 5 10 15 30 55 60

21. 8 13 20 33 46 57

22. 4 8 9 11 15 21

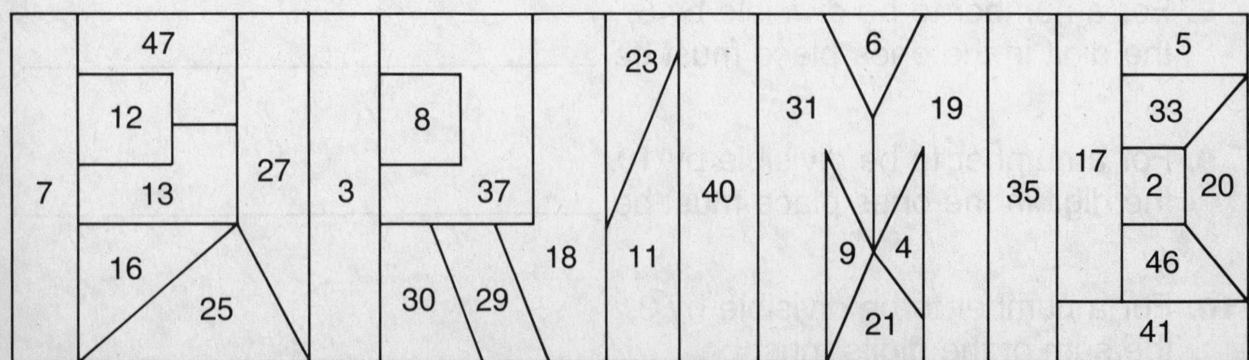

NAME ____________________

SHARPEN YOUR SKILLS

Greatest Common Factor

Find the common factors of each pair of numbers.
Circle the greatest common factor.

1. 4 and 18 ____________________ **2.** 15 and 25 ____________________

3. 21 and 35 ____________________ **4.** 24 and 32 ____________________

5. 13 and 26 ____________________ **6.** 8 and 28 ____________________

7. 12 and 42 ____________________ **8.** 18 and 81 ____________________

Find the GCF for each set of numbers.

9. 15, 20 _____ **10.** 9, 30 _____ **11.** 36, 18 _____

12. 49, 21 _____ **13.** 32, 40 _____ **14.** 33, 121 _____

15. 48, 96 _____ **16.** 22, 88 _____ **17.** 35, 105 _____

18. 72, 81 _____ **19.** 38, 57 _____ **20.** 64, 96 _____

Solve the problem.

21. Twenty band members will be arranged in rows with the same number in each row. Write all the possible ways they can be arranged.

____

____

NAME

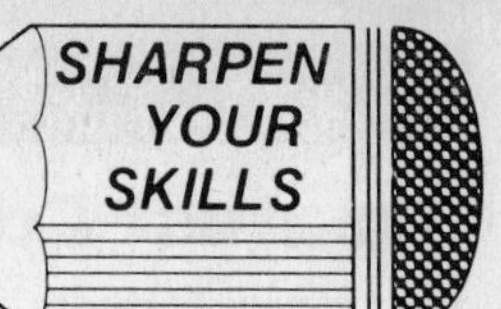

Try and Check

For each exercise, try and check to determine if the resulting number is always even, always odd, or can be either even or odd. Write *E, O,* or *E/O* for each number.

1. A number greater than 20 ______

2. Twice a number ______

3. The square of an even number ______

4. The square of an odd number ______

5. The sum of three even numbers ______

6. The sum of two odd numbers ______

7. The sum of two even numbers and an odd number ______

8. The product of two even numbers and an odd number ______

9. Three times your age ______

10. The year you were born plus your age ______

11. A number that divides into your age ______

12. The product of three odd numbers ______

Try and check to tell whether each number is composite. Write *Yes* if the number is composite and *No* if it is not.

13. 63 ______

14. 83 ______

15. 67 ______

16. 87 ______

17. 101 ______

18. 1,383 ______

19. 278 ______

20. 1,895 ______

21. 79 ______

22. 1,957 ______

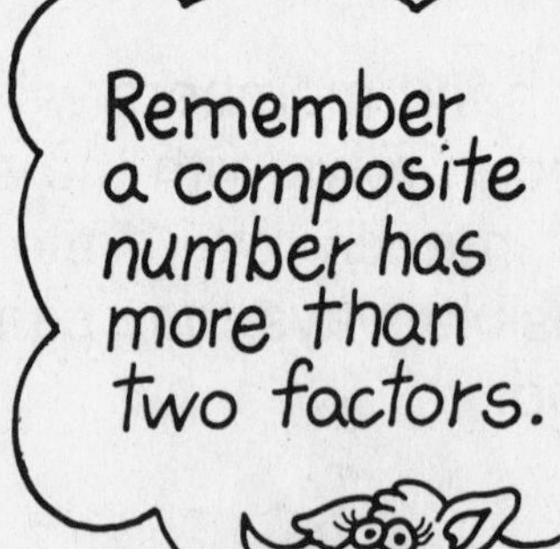

NAME

SHARPEN YOUR SKILLS

Equal Fractions

Write three fractions that are equal to the given fraction.

1. $\frac{2}{5}$ ______ **2.** $\frac{5}{8}$ ______ **3.** $\frac{1}{4}$ ______

4. $\frac{8}{10}$ ______ **5.** $\frac{4}{8}$ ______ **6.** $\frac{3}{4}$ ______

Write each fraction in lowest terms.

Connect the path of fractions equal to $\frac{1}{4}$.

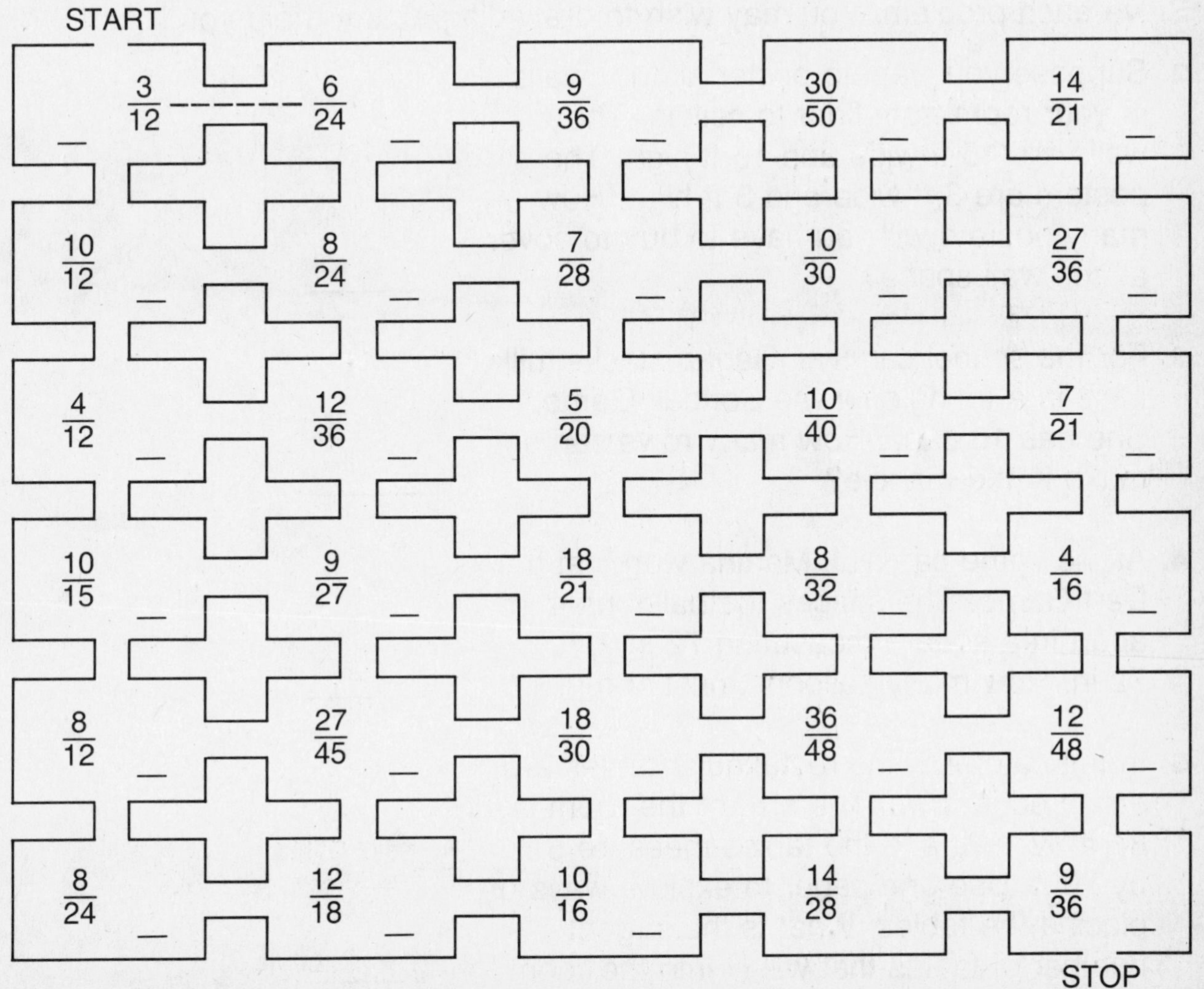

NAME

SHARPEN YOUR SKILLS

Find a Pattern

1. Find the pattern in the given dots and fill in the remaining square and rectangular numbers in the table.

	1st	2nd	3rd	4th	5th	6th	7th	8th	9th	10th
■	1	4	9							
▼	1	3	6							

Solve each problem. You may wish to draw diagrams to help you.

2. Suppose you want to poster all four walls in your room from floor to ceiling. The walls are 15 ft wide and 15 ft high. The posters are 3 ft wide and 3 ft high. How many posters will you have to buy to cover all the wall space? ______

3. For the school carnival, Regan stacks milk cans in a triangle for the Softball Game. She has 10 cans. How many rows can she make in the triangle? ______

4. At the same carnival, Martina works at the Dart Game. She spaces the balloons 4 in. apart in a square measuring 72 in. by 72 in. How many balloons must she use? ______

5. In the cafeteria, the rectangular tables are arranged in rows. The size of the room is 34 ft by 19 ft and the tables measure 5 ft by 10 ft. Use grid paper to explore ways of placing the tables. What is the largest number of tables that will fit into the room? ______

NAME

SHARPEN YOUR SKILLS

Multiples and Least Common Multiple

For Exercises 1–6, find the least common multiple (LCM) for each pair of numbers. Then tell whether you used mental math, paper and pencil, or a calculator to find the LCM. Write *M, P,* or *C.*

1. 10, 35 ________ **2.** 8, 7 ________ **3.** 5, 9 ________

4. 33, 27 ________ **5.** 6, 18 ________ **6.** 12, 4 ________

Mixed Practice Write the greatest common factor (GCF) and the LCM for each pair of numbers.

7. 8, 10 ________ **8.** 17, 3 ________ **9.** 24, 18 ________

When is your work like roast beef?

For each exercise, find the LCM. Cross out each box that contains an answer. Write the remaining letters in order in the blanks below the chart.

10. 3, 7 ______ **11.** 4, 5 ______ **12.** 2, 9 ______

13. 10, 12 ______ **14.** 15, 25 ______ **15.** 7, 12 ______

16. 3, 11 ______ **17.** 5, 8 ______ **18.** 2, 8 ______

19. 5, 9 ______ **20.** 7, 11 ______ **21.** 6, 7 ______

A	S	W	O	R	E	L	P	L	B
45	21	32	20	18	46	35	60	12	77
U	**D**	**K**	**O**	**M**	**N**	**W**	**E**	**T**	**F**
8	72	75	22	84	36	33	28	40	42

When it is ____ ____ ____ ____ ____ ____ ____ ____ .

NAME

SHARPEN YOUR SKILLS

Common Denominators

Rewrite each group of fractions using the least common denominator.

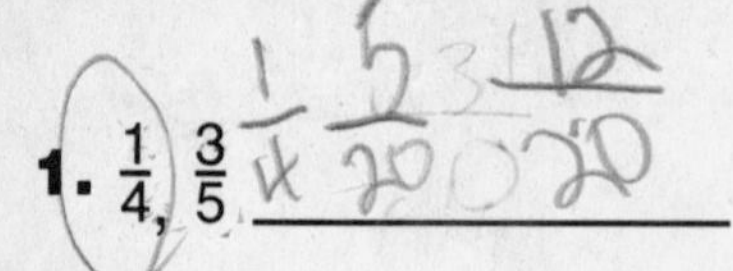

1. $\frac{1}{4}, \frac{3}{5}$ ________

2. $\frac{2}{7}, \frac{5}{6}$ ________

3. $\frac{4}{7}, \frac{1}{2}$ ________

4. $\frac{1}{3}, \frac{3}{4}$ ________

5. $\frac{2}{3}, \frac{1}{5}$ ________

6. $\frac{2}{9}, \frac{1}{6}$ ________

7. $\frac{3}{4}, \frac{5}{6}$ ________

8. $\frac{7}{8}, \frac{3}{5}$ ________

9. $\frac{4}{5}, \frac{1}{9}$ ________

10. $\frac{3}{8}, \frac{5}{6}, \frac{2}{3}$ ________

11. $\frac{1}{2}, \frac{1}{4}, \frac{5}{8}$ ________

12. $\frac{3}{10}, \frac{1}{3}, \frac{5}{6}$ ________

13. $\frac{3}{4}, \frac{1}{6}, \frac{2}{3}$ ________

Solve each problem.

The distances traveled during a mountain hiking trip are given. For each exercise, write the fractions with the least common denominator.

14. Monday: $\frac{2}{3}$ mile ________

Tuesday: $\frac{2}{5}$ mile ________

15. Wednesday: $\frac{3}{4}$ mile ________

Thursday: $\frac{7}{9}$ mile ________

NAME

SHARPEN YOUR SKILLS

Comparing and Ordering Fractions

Mental Math Compare the fractions. Use >, <, or =.

1. $\frac{1}{2} \bigcirc \frac{2}{3}$ **2.** $\frac{3}{5} \bigcirc \frac{1}{8}$ **3.** $\frac{5}{6} \bigcirc \frac{10}{12}$

4. $\frac{4}{5} \bigcirc \frac{1}{6}$ **5.** $\frac{1}{5} \bigcirc \frac{2}{10}$ **6.** $\frac{1}{5} \bigcirc \frac{1}{4}$

7. $\frac{5}{6} \bigcirc \frac{3}{7}$ **8.** $\frac{6}{8} \bigcirc \frac{3}{4}$ **9.** $\frac{4}{5} \bigcirc \frac{8}{10}$

10. $\frac{4}{7} \bigcirc \frac{5}{8}$ **11.** $\frac{7}{12} \bigcirc \frac{6}{11}$ **12.** $\frac{19}{38} \bigcirc \frac{1}{2}$

Rewrite the fractions in order from least to greatest.

13. $\frac{5}{6}, \frac{1}{6}, \frac{3}{6}$ ________________ **14.** $\frac{5}{8}, \frac{1}{4}, \frac{3}{5}$ ________________

15. $\frac{1}{3}, \frac{1}{4}, \frac{5}{12}$ ________________ **16.** $\frac{2}{3}, \frac{3}{4}, \frac{5}{6}$ ________________

17. $\frac{3}{8}, \frac{4}{16}, \frac{7}{11}$ ________________ **18.** $\frac{5}{12}, \frac{4}{9}, \frac{1}{3}$ ________________

Solve each problem.

19. During a hiking trip Joyce hiked $\frac{2}{3}$ mile and Marco hiked $\frac{5}{6}$ mile. Who hiked farther? ________________

20. Sue hiked $\frac{3}{5}$ mile, Allen hiked $\frac{3}{4}$ mile, and Jimmy hiked $\frac{1}{2}$ mile.

List the distances in order from least to greatest. ________________

NAME

SHARPEN YOUR SKILLS

Mixed Numbers and Improper Fractions

Compare. Use <, >, or =.

1. $3\frac{1}{2} \bigcirc 3\frac{1}{4}$

2. $1\frac{1}{6} \bigcirc 1\frac{5}{6}$

3. $7\frac{1}{2} \bigcirc 7\frac{2}{4}$

4. $8\frac{2}{3} \bigcirc 8\frac{1}{2}$

5. $6\frac{3}{4} \bigcirc 6\frac{2}{3}$

6. $\frac{15}{4} \bigcirc \frac{11}{3}$

Write in order from least to greatest.

7. $3\frac{1}{8}, 3\frac{3}{4}, 3\frac{1}{2}$ __________

8. $\frac{13}{3}, \frac{13}{6}, \frac{13}{2}$ __________

9. $2\frac{3}{5}, \frac{17}{5}, \frac{10}{5}$ __________

Write an improper fraction for each mixed number, or write a mixed number for each improper fraction.

10. $1\frac{1}{3} =$ _____

11. $2\frac{1}{2} =$ _____

12. $\frac{80}{12} =$ _____

13. $\frac{17}{12} =$ _____

14. $8\frac{2}{3} =$ _____

15. $6\frac{1}{5} =$ _____

16. $3\frac{1}{3} =$ _____

17. $\frac{43}{14} =$ _____

18. $4\frac{1}{2} =$ _____

19. $9\frac{1}{3} =$ _____

20. $6\frac{5}{8} =$ _____

21. $5\frac{2}{5} =$ _____

22. $6\frac{3}{8} =$ _____

23. $8\frac{1}{2} =$ _____

24. $\frac{11}{3} =$ _____

25. $\frac{60}{9} =$ _____

26. $\frac{76}{10} =$ _____

27. $2\frac{4}{5} =$ _____

NAME

SHARPEN YOUR SKILLS

Estimating Sums and Differences

Tell if each fraction is >, <, or = to $\frac{1}{2}$.

1. $\frac{5}{8} \bigcirc \frac{1}{2}$
2. $\frac{3}{5} \bigcirc \frac{1}{2}$
3. $\frac{7}{10} \bigcirc \frac{1}{2}$
4. $\frac{1}{4} \bigcirc \frac{1}{2}$
5. $\frac{3}{8} \bigcirc \frac{1}{2}$
6. $\frac{3}{16} \bigcirc \frac{1}{2}$
7. $\frac{3}{4} \bigcirc \frac{1}{2}$
8. $\frac{5}{12} \bigcirc \frac{1}{2}$

Round each mixed number to the nearest whole number.

9. $2\frac{1}{3}$ _____
10. $5\frac{2}{5}$ _____
11. $1\frac{4}{5}$ _____
12. $4\frac{11}{12}$ _____
13. $7\frac{2}{5}$ _____
14. $1\frac{3}{4}$ _____
15. $8\frac{7}{8}$ _____
16. $3\frac{3}{10}$ _____

Estimate each sum or difference. Round mixed numbers to the nearest whole number.

17. $1\frac{3}{5} + 6\frac{7}{9}$
18. $2\frac{7}{8} + 3\frac{1}{4}$
19. $2\frac{1}{4} - 1\frac{9}{10}$
20. $8\frac{5}{12} - 2\frac{4}{5}$
21. $3\frac{7}{10} + 7\frac{5}{6}$
22. $5\frac{3}{8} - 2\frac{1}{6}$

Critical Thinking A fraction is equal to $\frac{1}{3}$ if the denominator is three times the numerator. Explain how you can tell if a fraction is less than $\frac{1}{3}$.

_____

_____

_____

Use after pages 238–241.

NAME

SHARPEN YOUR SKILLS

Adding Fractions

Tell whether you would use mental math or paper and pencil to find each sum. Be sure to give answers in lowest terms.

1. $\frac{1}{5} + \frac{2}{3}$ ______

2. $\frac{1}{6} + \frac{1}{4}$ ______

3. $\frac{2}{7} + \frac{1}{4}$ ______

4. $\frac{4}{5} + \frac{5}{6}$ ______

5. $\frac{1}{2} + \frac{3}{7}$ ______

6. $\frac{2}{5} + \frac{3}{4}$ ______

7. $\frac{5}{6} + \frac{1}{3}$ ______

8. $\frac{4}{5} + \frac{3}{7}$ ______

9. $\frac{2}{3} + \frac{1}{6} + \frac{3}{8} =$ ______

10. $\frac{1}{2} + \frac{3}{10} + \frac{2}{5} =$ ______

11. $\frac{1}{3} + \frac{3}{4} + \frac{1}{2} =$ ______

12. $\frac{5}{9} + \frac{2}{3} + \frac{1}{2} =$ ______

Solve the problem.

13. Of all the band members, $\frac{1}{3}$ joined last year and $\frac{1}{5}$ joined this year. What fraction of the band members joined in the last two years? ______

NAME

SHARPEN YOUR SKILLS

Subtracting Fractions

What kind of snake is good at math?

To find out, subtract. Find your answer below. Cross out the letter in the box with that answer. The remaining letters solve the riddle. Write them in order on the blanks.

1. $\frac{3}{4} - \frac{1}{8}$

2. $\frac{5}{6} - \frac{1}{4}$

3. $\frac{2}{3} - \frac{1}{7}$

4. $\frac{1}{2} - \frac{1}{3}$

5. $\frac{2}{9} - \frac{1}{6}$

6. $\frac{1}{6} - \frac{1}{7}$

7. $\frac{2}{3} - \frac{1}{4}$

8. $\frac{7}{10} - \frac{3}{5}$

9. $\frac{3}{5} - \frac{3}{10}$

10. $\frac{7}{8} - \frac{1}{2}$

11. $\frac{5}{6} - \frac{2}{3}$

12. $\frac{4}{13} - \frac{5}{26}$

13. $\frac{5}{6} - \frac{3}{4}$

14. $\frac{5}{9} - \frac{1}{3}$

15. $\frac{3}{8} - \frac{1}{6}$

16. $\frac{4}{5} - \frac{2}{3}$

K	B	A	H	L	G	S	T	O	N	X	C
$\frac{1}{6}$	$\frac{5}{8}$	$\frac{3}{7}$	$\frac{1}{6}$	$\frac{1}{10}$	$\frac{1}{18}$	$\frac{7}{12}$	$\frac{1}{12}$	$\frac{11}{21}$	$\frac{2}{5}$	$\frac{5}{24}$	$\frac{2}{15}$
I	**P**	**A**	**U**	**D**	**D**	**Y**	**E**	**F**	**R**	**!**	**U**
$\frac{2}{9}$	$\frac{3}{8}$	$\frac{5}{6}$	$\frac{5}{12}$	$\frac{3}{11}$	$\frac{1}{24}$	$\frac{1}{42}$	$\frac{1}{9}$	$\frac{3}{10}$	$\frac{1}{4}$	$\frac{11}{12}$	$\frac{3}{26}$

____ ____ ____ ____ ____ ____ ____ ____

NAME

SHARPEN YOUR SKILLS

Work Backward

Find the greatest unit fraction less than each of the following.

1. $\frac{5}{12}$ ________ **2.** $\frac{4}{6}$ ________ **3.** $\frac{3}{16}$ ________

4. $\frac{4}{15}$ ________ **5.** $\frac{2}{9}$ ________ **6.** $\frac{6}{7}$ ________

7. $\frac{4}{13}$ ________ **8.** $\frac{13}{23}$ ________ **9.** $\frac{2}{11}$ ________

Write each fraction as the sum of unit fractions with different denominators.

10. $\frac{8}{12}$ ________ **11.** $\frac{2}{3}$ ________ **12.** $\frac{9}{20}$ ________

13. $\frac{11}{24}$ ________ **14.** $\frac{12}{12}$ ________ **15.** $\frac{7}{10}$ ________

16. $\frac{4}{9}$ ________ **17.** $\frac{3}{5}$ ________ **18.** $\frac{9}{24}$ ________

Use after pages 248–249.

NAME

SHARPEN YOUR SKILLS

Adding Mixed Numbers

Estimate each sum. Then add.

1. $3\frac{4}{9} + 7\frac{7}{9}$

2. $8\frac{2}{3} + 5\frac{2}{3}$

3. $2\frac{3}{5} + 8\frac{2}{5}$

4. $1\frac{5}{8} + 7\frac{5}{8}$

5. $10\frac{2}{3} + 3\frac{4}{7}$

6. $6\frac{2}{9} + 4\frac{5}{6}$

7. $2\frac{3}{4} + \frac{7}{10}$

8. $\frac{5}{6} + 6\frac{3}{8}$

9. $5\frac{1}{3} + 6\frac{3}{4} =$ __________

10. $6\frac{4}{15} + 8\frac{3}{5} =$ __________

Solve each problem.

11. The music class practiced two songs before a recital. The first song lasted $2\frac{7}{12}$ minutes and the second song lasted $3\frac{5}{6}$ minutes. How long did it take to perform the two songs? __________

12. The band members practiced for $2\frac{1}{3}$ hours on Monday and $3\frac{3}{4}$ hours on Tuesday. How many hours did they practice in all? __________

NAME

SHARPEN YOUR SKILLS

Subtracting Mixed Numbers

Subtract. Connect the answers from START to FINISH. Circle the correct FINISH.

1. $12\frac{3}{7} - 7\frac{4}{5}$

2. $13 - 7\frac{7}{15}$

3. $18\frac{4}{9} - 7\frac{5}{6}$

4. $14\frac{3}{5} - 12\frac{2}{3}$

5. $7\frac{1}{7} - 3\frac{1}{3}$

6. $13\frac{1}{4} - 9\frac{4}{9}$

7. $17 - 9\frac{1}{4}$

8. $6\frac{1}{8} - 2\frac{3}{4}$

9. $8\frac{3}{10} - 1\frac{2}{5}$

10. $19\frac{1}{6} - 7\frac{7}{8}$

11. $7\frac{9}{14} - 2\frac{1}{2}$

12. $5\frac{1}{3} - 2\frac{3}{4}$

13. $14\frac{2}{5} - 6\frac{2}{3}$

14. $11\frac{1}{3} - 1\frac{1}{6}$

15. $22\frac{1}{3} - 18\frac{1}{2}$

16. $21\frac{7}{10} - 9\frac{3}{4}$

$11\frac{11}{18}$	$2\frac{14}{15}$	$3\frac{29}{36}$	$7\frac{3}{4}$	$3\frac{3}{8}$	$5\frac{9}{10}$	$12\frac{5}{8}$	FINISH
$10\frac{11}{18}$	$1\frac{14}{15}$	$3\frac{17}{21}$	$3\frac{5}{9}$	$6\frac{9}{10}$	$11\frac{9}{25}$	$2\frac{5}{6}$	FINISH
$5\frac{8}{15}$	$10\frac{13}{18}$	$2\frac{11}{15}$	$3\frac{7}{12}$	$11\frac{7}{24}$	$3\frac{5}{6}$	$11\frac{19}{20}$	FINISH
START $4\frac{22}{35}$	$5\frac{7}{15}$	$5\frac{11}{14}$	$5\frac{1}{7}$	$5\frac{1}{7}$	$10\frac{1}{6}$	$9\frac{1}{2}$	FINISH
$2\frac{14}{15}$	$8\frac{7}{8}$	$1\frac{3}{5}$	$5\frac{2}{3}$	$2\frac{7}{12}$	$7\frac{11}{15}$	$7\frac{2}{3}$	FINISH

NAME

SHARPEN YOUR SKILLS

Too Much or Too Little Information

If there is too much information given, cross out the unnecessary information and give the answer. If not enough information is given, tell what facts are missing.

1. Mrs. Garcia drove to Midvale once a week for 7 weeks. Each round trip of 150 miles took $2\frac{3}{4}$ hours. How many miles did she travel altogether if she used $6\frac{1}{2}$ gallons of gas on each trip?

2. Each month Sarah used 24 gallons of gasoline and spent \$60 for parking, \$20.80 for auto insurance, and \$2 for motor oil. How much did she spend in $8\frac{1}{2}$ months for gasoline?

3. Glen needs a new tire for his bicycle. He has $\frac{3}{4}$ of the cost of the tire. How much more money does he need?

4. Sarah jogs $\frac{3}{4}$ hour on each of 5 days of the week. On the other 2 days, she jogs 2 hours a day. How many days a week does she jog?

5. Mr. Garcia spends about \$18.00 each time he fills his gas tank. He can drive about $4\frac{1}{2}$ hours on a full tank of gas. This amount of time includes $\frac{3}{4}$ hour when the gas gauge reads empty. How long can he drive on a full tank of gas before the gauge reads empty?

6. Glen spent $\frac{1}{3}$ of his allowance on a basket for his bike. How much money did he have left from his allowance?

7. Sarah paid \$2.50 in tolls and \$4 for 2 hours of parking. At the same rate, how much would she spend for $6\frac{1}{2}$ hours of parking?

SHARPEN YOUR SKILLS

Meaning of Multiplication of Fractions

A nature club is spending a week hiking in the mountains. The hikers can hike 3 miles per hour. Make a table that shows how far they walked.

1.

hours	0	1	2	3	4	5
miles						

2. Make a table that shows hours and half hours from 0 to 3 hours.

hours	0		1		2		3
miles	0		3		6		9

Complete each table for the number of hours and the number of miles the hikers walked.

3.

hours	0	$\frac{1}{3}$	$\frac{2}{3}$	1	$1\frac{1}{3}$	$1\frac{2}{3}$	2
miles	0			3			6

4.

hours	0	$\frac{1}{4}$	$\frac{1}{2}$	$\frac{3}{4}$	1	$1\frac{1}{4}$	$1\frac{1}{2}$	$1\frac{3}{4}$	2
miles	0				3				6

Some days the club slowed down or was able to go faster. Complete each table for the amount of miles the hikers walked according to the given information.

5.

hours	0	$\frac{1}{2}$	1	$1\frac{1}{2}$	2	$2\frac{1}{2}$	3
miles		1			4		

6.

hours	0	$\frac{1}{3}$	$\frac{2}{3}$	1	$1\frac{1}{3}$	$1\frac{2}{3}$	2
miles				4			

Problem Solving One morning the club members hiked 5 miles per hour.

7. How far would they hike in 2 hours? ______________

8. How far would they hike in $3\frac{3}{4}$ hours? ______________

9. How far would they hike in $2\frac{1}{2}$ hours? ______________

10. How far would they hike in $5\frac{1}{2}$ hours? ______________

Use after pages 272–275.

NAME

SHARPEN YOUR SKILLS

Multiplying Fractions

Why does a cabbage always win a race with a carrot?

To find out, multiply. Write your answer in lowest terms. **Remember** to use the shortcut method when possible. Write each letter above its matching answer. Some answers are given more than once.

1. $\frac{1}{2} \times \frac{3}{4} =$ ________ D

2. $\frac{3}{4} \times \frac{1}{5} =$ ________ S

3. $\frac{7}{10} \times \frac{7}{10} =$ ________ A

4. $\frac{1}{4} \times \frac{2}{3} =$ ________ L

5. $\frac{1}{2} \times \frac{4}{5} =$ ________ S

6. $\frac{1}{3} \times \frac{6}{7} =$ ________ W

7. $\frac{3}{10} \times \frac{2}{3} =$ ________ E

8. $\frac{5}{6} \times \frac{5}{8} =$ ________ T

9. $\frac{3}{4} \times \frac{2}{5} =$ ________ Y

10. $\frac{7}{8} \times \frac{3}{4} =$ ________ I

11. $\frac{2}{3} \times \frac{5}{8} =$ ________ H

12. $\frac{1}{3} \times \frac{4}{5} =$ ________ A

___ ___ ' ___

$\frac{21}{32}$ $\frac{25}{48}$ $\frac{3}{20}$

___ ___ ___ ___ ___ ___

$\frac{4}{15}$ $\frac{1}{6}$ $\frac{2}{7}$ $\frac{49}{100}$ $\frac{3}{10}$ $\frac{2}{5}$

___ ___ ___ ___ ___.

$\frac{49}{100}$ $\frac{5}{12}$ $\frac{1}{5}$ $\frac{4}{15}$ $\frac{3}{8}$

NAME

SHARPEN YOUR SKILLS

Multiplying Mixed Numbers

Multiply. **Remember** to change the mixed numbers to fractions. To complete the message, cross out each box that contains a correct answer.

1. $2 \times 1\frac{1}{2} =$ ____ **2.** $1\frac{1}{2} \times 3 =$ ____ **3.** $3 \times 2\frac{2}{3} =$ ____

4. $\frac{1}{3} \times 2\frac{1}{3} =$ ____ **5.** $1\frac{1}{3} \times 12 =$ ____ **6.** $\frac{3}{4} \times 5\frac{1}{3} =$ ____

7. $1\frac{2}{3} \times 1\frac{1}{4} =$ ____ **8.** $2\frac{1}{4} \times \frac{1}{2} =$ ____ **9.** $\frac{5}{6} \times 2\frac{2}{5} =$ ____

Estimation. Find a range. Then multiply.

10. $1\frac{1}{2} \times 15 =$ ____

Range: ________

11. $2\frac{1}{2} \times 3\frac{3}{5} =$ ____

Range: ________

12. $1\frac{1}{2} \times 2\frac{1}{4} =$ ____

Range: ________

13. $2\frac{1}{4} \times 1\frac{2}{5} =$ ____

Range: ________

14. $3\frac{1}{2} \times 2\frac{1}{3} =$ ____

Range: ________

15. $1\frac{3}{8} \times \frac{1}{3} =$ ____

Range: ________

HAPPINESS IS

A	**F**	**S**	**G**	**B**	**U**	**H**	**C**	**O**	**M**	**I**
8	$\frac{11}{24}$	7	3	16	24	9	4	$3\frac{3}{20}$	$\frac{3}{11}$	$2\frac{1}{12}$
J	**M**	**K**	**E**	**P**	**T**	**R**	**N**	**L**	**!**	**D**
$1\frac{1}{8}$	$1\frac{17}{18}$	$3\frac{3}{8}$	6	$22\frac{1}{2}$	$4\frac{1}{2}$	14	$8\frac{1}{6}$	2	$4\frac{3}{5}$	$\frac{7}{9}$

NAME

Use Alternate Strategies

SHARPEN YOUR SKILLS

Solve each problem.

1. A row of 60 peas is about 1 foot long. How many peas would be in a row that was 288 inches?

2. Show how to solve Exercise 1 using another strategy.

3. If 200 peas weigh $\frac{3}{5}$ pound, how many peas would be in 36 pounds?

4. Show how to solve Exercise 2 using another strategy.

5. Peter has 24 coins. In this group of coins there are only pennies and quarters. The total amount of money is $3.60. How many pennies and quarters does he have?

6. If Peter exchanged a quarter for nickels, how many coins would Peter have?

7. Peter has a total of 24 coins. This group includes all types of coins, except half dollars and silver dollars. What is the greatest amount of money he can have?

8. Show how to solve Exercise 7 using another strategy.

9. Peter has $3.60 in coins. What is the smallest number of coins, excluding silver dollars, that he can have?

10. Show how to solve Exercise 8 using another strategy.

NAME

SHARPEN YOUR SKILLS

Mental Math: Properties

Use mental math to find each answer.
Remember to look for reciprocals.

1. $2\frac{1}{2} + 3\frac{3}{4} + 1\frac{1}{2}$

2. $3\frac{1}{3} \times 6$

3. $5\frac{1}{4} + 3\frac{3}{4} + 1\frac{1}{2}$

4. $\frac{2}{5} + 1\frac{1}{5} + 2\frac{1}{5}$

5. $3 \times 2\frac{1}{3}$

6. $5 \times 3\frac{1}{5}$

7. $4 \times 3\frac{1}{4} + 2 \times 1\frac{1}{5}$

8. $6\frac{3}{4} + 1\frac{1}{4}$

9. $5\frac{9}{10} + 4\frac{1}{10}$

Critical Thinking Solve each problem.

10. How many 2-foot lengths of pipe can be cut from 3 lengths that are $2\frac{1}{2}$ feet, $5\frac{3}{4}$ feet, and $3\frac{1}{4}$ feet?

11. Look at Exercise 10. How much pipe will be left over?

12. What is the total length of 3 pieces of pipe that are $3\frac{3}{4}$ feet, $4\frac{1}{2}$ feet, and $5\frac{3}{4}$ feet?

13. Look at Exercise 12. How many 4-foot lengths can you cut from these 3 pieces?

14. Which will yield more 5-foot lengths—a single piece 15 feet long or 2 9-foot pieces totaling 18 feet?

NAME

Choose an Operation

SHARPEN YOUR SKILLS

First write the operation needed to solve each problem. Then solve the problem.

1. Terry is an artist who makes collages. He uses metal wire and other objects. He has three pieces of wire that are $2\frac{3}{4}$ inches, $3\frac{1}{8}$ inches, and $4\frac{5}{8}$ inches. How much space does he need to place them end to end?

______ ______

2. Terry has $22\frac{5}{8}$ inches of ribbon. He cut $12\frac{1}{2}$ inches off to make a collage. How much ribbon does he have left?

______ ______

3. Terry made a frame for his finished collage. The collage is $33\frac{1}{2}$ inches wide. The frame is $3\frac{3}{4}$ inches. What is the total width of the framed collage? **Remember** that the frame goes all around the collage.

______ ______

4. In order to hang the collage from its middle, Terry needs to know what half the width is. What is half the width including the frame?

______ ______

5. Janice needs to know how many postcards placed side by side will fit on a wall space that is 36 inches long. If each postcard is 6 inches long, how many will fit?

______ ______

6. If the postcards were half as long and the space were 27 inches, how many would fit?

______ ______

Use after pages 288–289.

NAME

SHARPEN YOUR SKILLS

Meaning of Division of Fractions

Find each quotient. Use the ruler to help you.

1. $1\frac{3}{4} \div \frac{1}{4}$

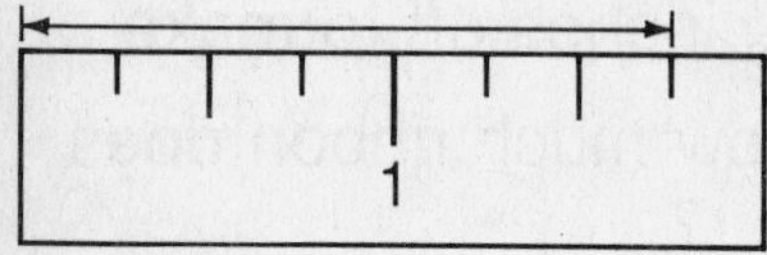

______

2. $1\frac{1}{2} \div \frac{1}{8}$

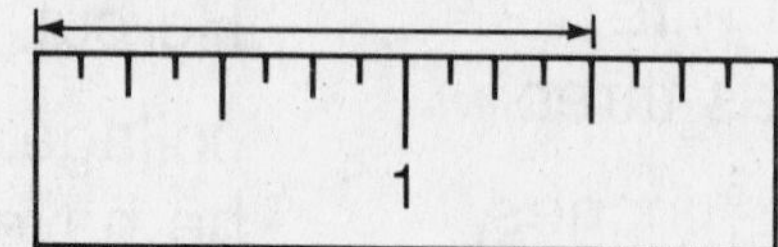

______

3. $\frac{5}{8} \div \frac{1}{8}$

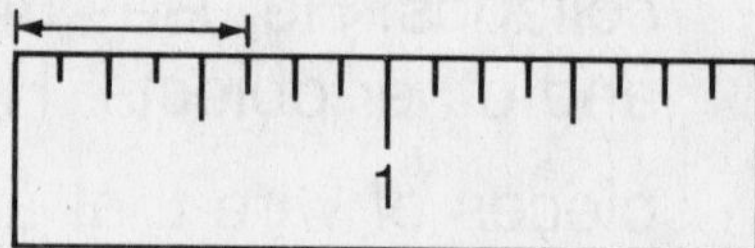

______

4. $1\frac{1}{2} \div \frac{3}{8}$

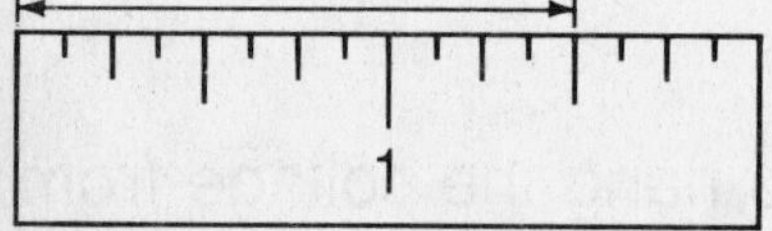

______

5. $1\frac{1}{8} \div \frac{3}{8}$

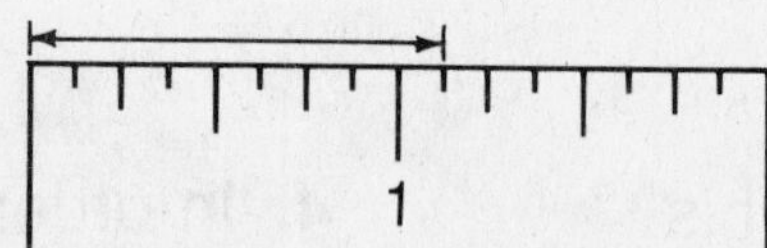

______

6. $1\frac{1}{2} \div \frac{1}{4}$

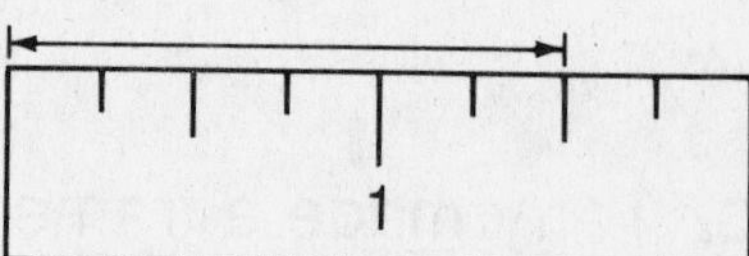

______

Use a calculator or pencil and paper to find each quotient.

7. $6 \div \frac{3}{4}$ ______

8. $9 \div \frac{3}{10}$ ______

9. $12\frac{1}{4} \div 1\frac{3}{4}$ ______

10. $5\frac{5}{8} \div \frac{5}{8}$ ______

11. $13\frac{1}{2} \div 2\frac{1}{4}$ ______

12. $9 \div 1\frac{4}{5}$ ______

13. $12 \div \frac{3}{10}$ ______

14. $8 \div 3\frac{1}{5}$ ______

15. $2\frac{2}{8} \div \frac{2}{5}$ ______

NAME

SHARPEN YOUR SKILLS

Dividing Fractions and Mixed Numbers

What is black and white and red all over?

To find out, find the quotient. Then cross out each square that contains a correct answer.

1. $4 \div 1\frac{7}{8} =$ ____

2. $4\frac{2}{3} \div 3 =$ ____

3. $5 \div 2\frac{3}{4} =$ ____

4. $4\frac{1}{2} \div 2 =$ ____

5. $8 \div 4\frac{3}{4} =$ ____

6. $\frac{3}{5} \div 1\frac{1}{4} =$ ____

7. $\frac{5}{6} \div 2\frac{1}{3} =$ ____

8. $2\frac{2}{5} \div 3\frac{1}{5} =$ ____

9. $3\frac{1}{3} \div 4\frac{1}{2} =$ ____

10. $3\frac{1}{2} \div 3\frac{1}{2} =$ ____

11. $2\frac{1}{3} \div 2\frac{4}{5} =$ ____

12. $6\frac{4}{5} \div 2\frac{1}{2} =$ ____

C	**A**	**K**	**M**	**B**	**D**	**L**	**O**	**J**	**U**	**S**	**N**	**H**
$\frac{3}{4}$	3	$1\frac{5}{9}$	$2\frac{18}{25}$	$1\frac{11}{12}$	$1\frac{13}{19}$	$\frac{3}{10}$	1	$\frac{5}{14}$	$\frac{4}{13}$	$\frac{28}{51}$	$1\frac{9}{11}$	$\frac{44}{57}$
I	**F**	**T**	**N**	**G**	**Q**	**Z**	**E**	**V**	**B**	**P**	**R**	**A**
$\frac{1}{2}$	$2\frac{1}{4}$	$\frac{12}{25}$	$2\frac{4}{5}$	$\frac{5}{7}$	$\frac{20}{27}$	$\frac{8}{11}$	$1\frac{6}{13}$	$2\frac{2}{15}$	$3\frac{1}{2}$	$\frac{5}{6}$	$1\frac{1}{20}$	$4\frac{1}{3}$

____ ______________ ______________

NAME

SHARPEN YOUR SKILLS

Customary Units of Length, Area, and Volume

Find each missing number.
Remember to multiply when changing to a smaller unit and divide when changing to a larger unit.

1. 3 ft = ____________ in.

2. 2 yd = ____________ in.

3. 2 ft 3 in. = ____________ in.

4. 15 in. = ______ ft ______ in.

5. 37 in. = ______ ft ______ in.

6. 2 yd 5 in. = ______ ft ______ in.

7. 10,560 ft = ____________ mi

8. 1 cu yd = ____________ cu ft

What always happens at the end of a dry spell?

For each set of measures, express one in the same terms as the other. If the two measures are equal, circle the letter above them. The circled letters will answer the question.

C	I	O	T	S	O
27 in. 2 ft 2 in.	9 ft 3 yd	30 in. 10 ft	4 yd 12 ft	1 ft 4 in. 17 in.	5 yd 15 in.

R	A	B	I	N	S
2 mi 10,560 ft	5 ft 1 yd 2 ft	21 in. 7 ft	12 ft 4 yd	5 ft 60 in.	1 ft 1 in. 13 in.

Use after pages 306–307.

NAME

SHARPEN YOUR SKILLS

Estimating and Measuring in the Customary System

Use the line segments below to complete the table.
Write the measure of each segment in the unit indicated.

$\overline{AB}$ $1\frac{1}{4}$ "

$\overline{CD}$ $2\frac{3}{4}$ "

$\overline{EF}$ $3\frac{5}{16}$ "

$\overline{GH}$ $4\frac{3}{8}$ "

To nearest	$\overline{AB}$	$\overline{CD}$	$\overline{EF}$	$\overline{GH}$
inch	**1.**	**2.**	**3.**	**4.**
half inch	**5.**	**6.**	**7.**	**8.**
quarter inch	**9.**	**10.**	**11.**	**12.**
eighth inch	**13.**	**14.**	**15.**	**16.**

Estimate the length of each line segment.
Then measure the length with a ruler, and
write the measure to the nearest quarter inch.

17. ______

18. ______

19. ______

20. ______

21. ______

22. ______

SHARPEN YOUR SKILLS

Customary Units of Capacity and Weight

Circle the more sensible measure for each object.

1. A bowl of soup

1 c 1 qt

2. A casserole dish

2 qt 2 gal

3. A thermos

1 oz 1 qt

4. A rubber ball

17 oz 17 lb

5. A telephone

4 lb 4 oz

6. A sack of onions

0.12 oz 12 lb

Give each equivalent measure.

7. 3 qt = ____________ pt

8. 8 c = ____________ pt

9. 2 gal = ____________ pt

10. 4 gal = _____ qt _____ pt

11. 10 c = _____ qt _____ pt

12. 13 pt = _____ qt _____ pt

13. 8 qt = _____ gal _____ qt

14. 12 pt = _____ gal _____ qt

15. 20 pt = _____ gal _____ qt

16. 2 lb = ____________ oz

17. 3 lb 4 oz = ____________ oz

18. 2 T = ____________ fl oz

19. 60 oz = _____ lb _____ oz

20. 43 oz = _____ lb _____ oz

21. 4 lb 6 oz = ____________ oz

22. 5 lb 6 oz = ____________ oz

Solve each problem.

23. Sandra canned 3 gallons of peaches. How many pints is this?

____

24. Sam cooked 12 pints of soup. How many quarts is this?

____

NAME

SHARPEN YOUR SKILLS

Choose an Operation

Solve each problem.

1. Nancy is making a pudding that calls for 12 pints of milk. How many quarts of milk will she have to open to make the pudding?

2. Julian bought 3 sacks of potatoes. Each sack weighed 19 pounds 7 ounces. How much did the potatoes weigh in all?

3. Lorraine is filling up a 5-gallon container with water. How many fluid ounces of water will be in the container when it is full?

4. Jaime, Kumiko, and Ned are sharing an order of cole slaw. The order weighs 1 pound 2 ounces. How much cole slaw will each of them have?

5. Rob took 3 quarts of water from Lorraine's 5-gallon container. How many quarts are left? How many pints?

6. If 36 people drink 1 cup of water each, how many quarts of water will be consumed? How many fluid ounces would that be?

7. A gallon of water weighs 8 pounds. How many ounces do 3 gallons of water weigh?

8. How many quarts of water would weigh 1,432 pounds?

NAME

SHARPEN YOUR SKILLS

Metric Units of Length, Area, and Volume

Find each missing number.

1. 25 cm = ________ m

2. 3 m = ________ dm

3. 3.7 dm = ________ m

4. 4,000 m = ________ km

5. 2.4 m = ________ mm

6. 354 m = ________ km

7. 340 hm = ________ m

8. 410 mm = ________ cm

9. 4,354 cm = ________ hm

10. 3.5 km = ________ dm

11. 15 m = ________ cm

12. 12,000 m = ________ km

Solve each problem.

13. A swimming pool is exactly 3 meters long, 3 meters wide, and 3 meters deep. How many cubic centimeters is this?

____

14. To buy a pool cover that must reach 100 centimeters beyond the edge on all sides, what must the area of the cover be in square centimeters?

____

NAME

SHARPEN YOUR SKILLS

Estimating and Measuring in the Metric System

Estimate the length of each segment in millimeters.
Then measure each item to the nearest millimeter.

1.  ______

2.  ______

3.  ______

4. 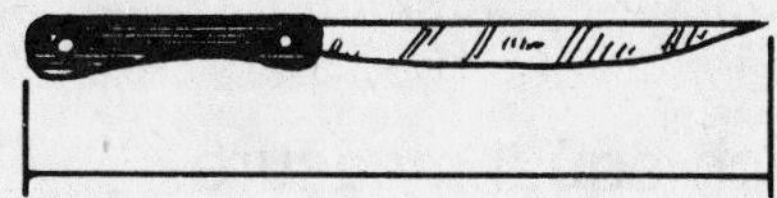 ______

Estimate the length of each segment in centimeters.
Then measure each item to the nearest centimeter.

5. 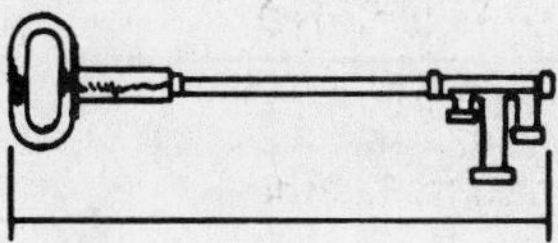 ______

6. 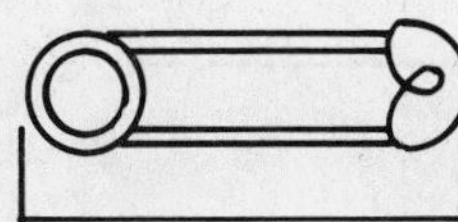 ______

7.  ______

8. 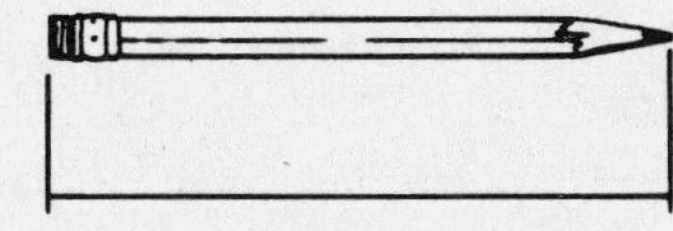 ______

Draw a segment for each of the following lengths.

9. 2.9 cm

10. 36 mm

11. 1.2 cm

12. 24 mm

Use after pages 320–321.

NAME

SHARPEN YOUR SKILLS

Metric Units of Capacity and Mass

Circle the more sensible measure for each object.

1. A pint of cream

500 mL 500 L

2. A garbage can

80 mL 80 L

3. A pitcher of water

1 mL 1 L

4. A watch

30 g 30 kg

5. An adult woman

54 g 54 kg

6. A steak

1 mg 1 kg

Give each equal measure.

7. 5,000 mL = ____________ L

8. 24,000 mL = ____________ L

9. 867 mL = ____________ L

10. 3L = ____________ mL

11. 7 L = ____________ mL

12. 3.47 L = ____________ mL

13. 6 kg = ____________ g

14. 54 kg = ____________ g

15. 2.7 kg = ____________ g

16. 2 g = ____________ kg

17. 62 g = ____________ kg

18. 1.25 g = ____________ kg

19. 4,000 g = ____________ kg

20. 3,900 g = ____________ kg

Solve each problem.

21. Dora baked 18 kilograms of bread for a bake sale. How many grams is this?

____

22. Dora's brother Tom baked 17,000 grams of rolls for the sale. How many kilograms is this?

____

NAME ____________

SHARPEN YOUR SKILLS

Time

Find each missing number.

1. 39 min = ________ sec

2. 5 h = ________ min

3. 864 h = ________ da

4. 1,980 sec = ________ min

5. 198 h = _____ da _____ h

6. 900 min = ________ h

7. 560 y = _____ centuries _____ y

8. 9 h 37 min = ________ min

9. 7 da = ________ h

10. 580 sec = _____ min _____ sec

Find each time.

11. from 9:54 P.M. to 11:01 P.M.

____

12. from 6:43 A.M. to 10:37 A.M.

____

13. from 7:29 A.M. to 4:44 P.M.

____

14. 3 h 17 min after 8:30 A.M.

____

Solve.

15.
```
   3 h 22 min
 + 5 h 12 min
 ------------
```

16.
```
   5 h 55 min
 + 8 h 34 min
 ------------
```

17.
```
   3 h 36 min
 − 1 h 48 min
 ------------
```

18.
```
   4 h 27 min
 − 2 h 56 min
 ------------
```

NAME

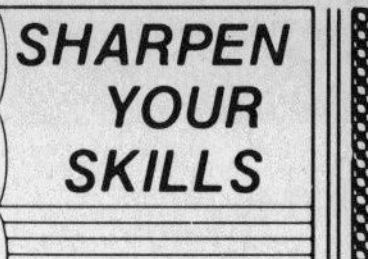

Use Data from a Table

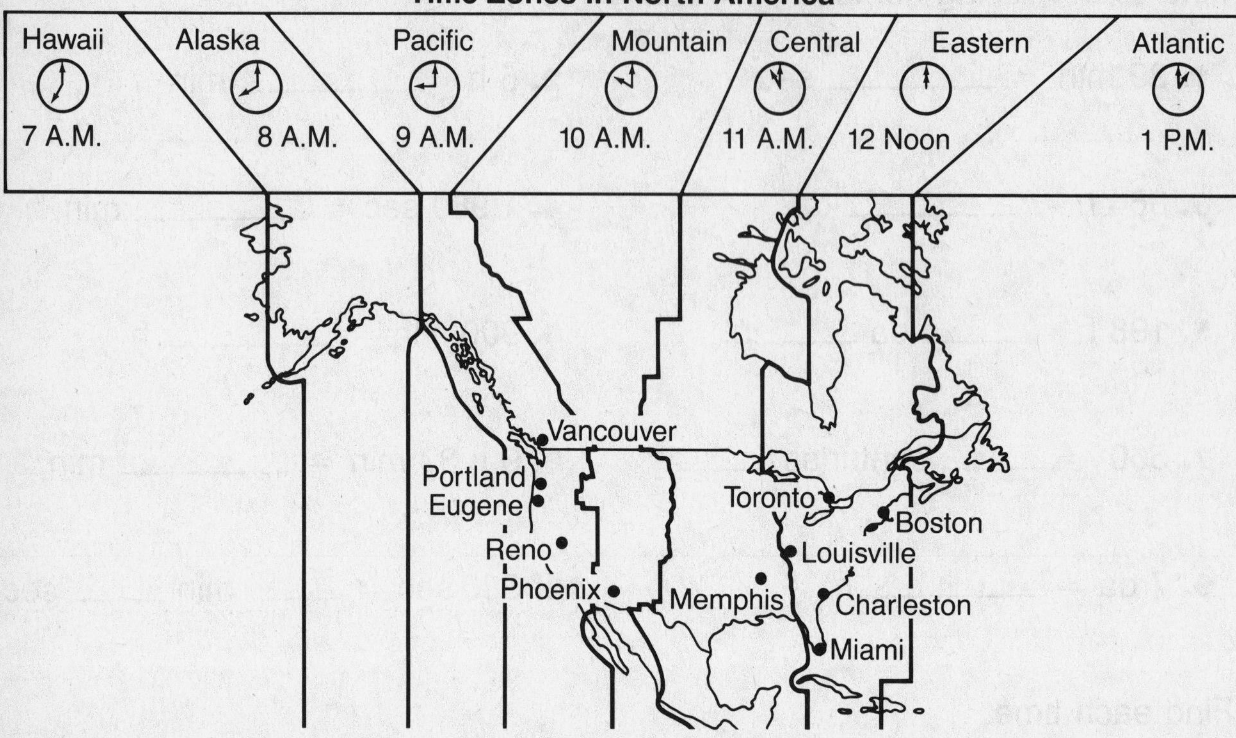

Would you set your watch forward or backward when flying between the following cities?

1. Toronto to Eugene ____________

2. Phoenix to Boston ____________

3. When it is 5:00 P.M. in Miami, what time is it in Memphis?

____

4. When it is 8:30 A.M. in Vancouver, what time is it in Reno?

____

Solve each problem.

5. Sylvia needs to make a long distance call to Portland. If she calls from Charleston at 2:00 P.M., what time is it in Portland?

____

6. Tim's flight leaves Reno at 1:20 P.M. What time is it in Louisville when the flight leaves?

____

NAME

SHARPEN YOUR SKILLS

Temperature

Circle the more sensible temperature.

1. A cold drink

5°C 50°C

2. Hot soup

85°C 15°C

3. A sunny day

25°C 85°C

4. An ice cube

0°C 32°C

5. Cold pizza

60°C 10°C

6. A lighted oven

100°C 50°C

7. Frozen juice

32°F 60°F

8. Warm pizza

75°F 50°F

9. A freezer

32°F 50°F

The graph at the right shows the temperatures for a 12-hour period.

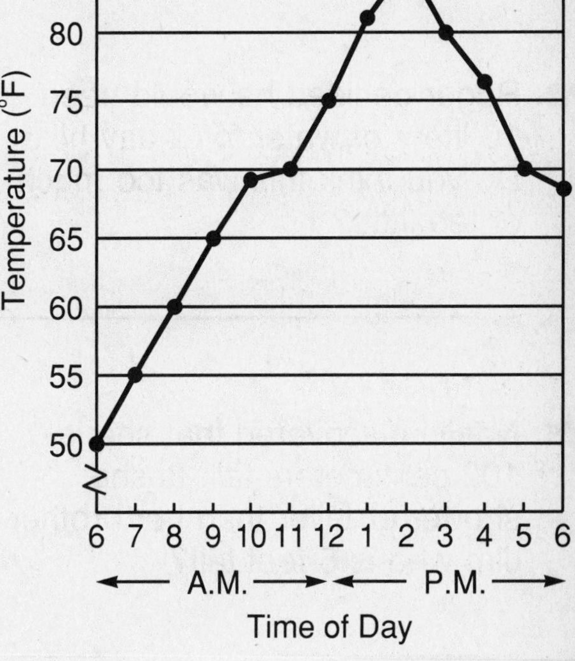

10. At what time was the temperature the highest? At what time was it the lowest?

__________ __________

11. Find the rise in temperature from 6:00 A.M. to 11:00 A.M.

____

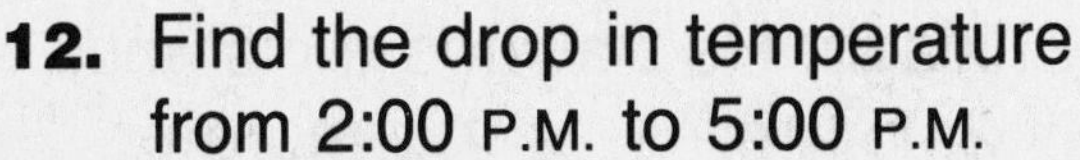

12. Find the drop in temperature from 2:00 P.M. to 5:00 P.M.

____

13. Find the difference in temperature from 6:00 A.M. to 3:00 P.M.

____

Use after pages 328–329.

NAME

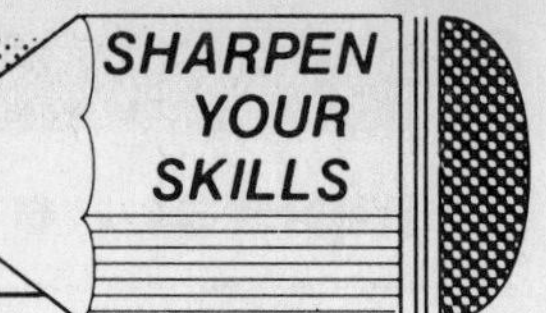

Give Sensible Answers

Solve each problem.
Remember to relate the sizes of customary and metric units.

1. Lawrence was driving at 80 kilometers per hour. If the speed limit is 55 miles per hour, was Lawrence speeding?

____

2. Natasha bought 12 kilograms of potatoes. Was this more or less than 20 pounds?

____

3. Roger decided he would need 10 liters of water for a day hike. Do you think this was too much or too little?

____

4. Roger was carrying a pack that weighed 25 pounds. Is this more or less than 18 kilograms?

____

5. Noelle discovered that she is 102 centimeters tall. Is she shorter or taller than her brother Jim who is 5 feet tall?

____

6. A soccer field is 110 meters long. Is this longer or shorter than a 300-foot football field?

____

7. Carmine bought 10 gallons of apple cider. About how many liters is this?

10 20 30 40

8. Lee flew from Los Angeles to Chicago. He traveled a distance of 2,054 miles. Is this more or less than 3,000 kilometers?

____

NAME

SHARPEN YOUR SKILLS

Perimeter

Find the perimeter of each polygon.

1.

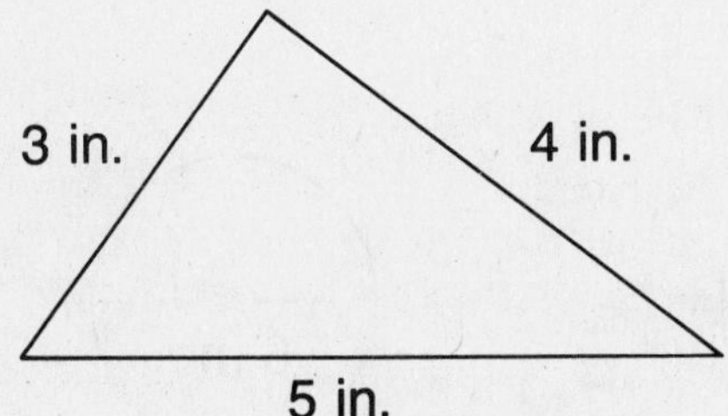

2.

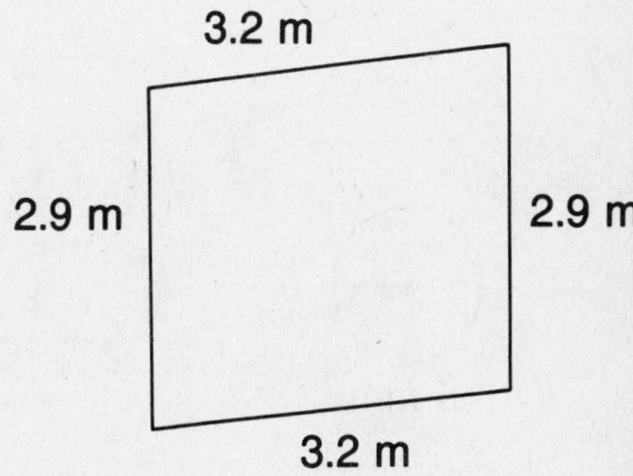

3.

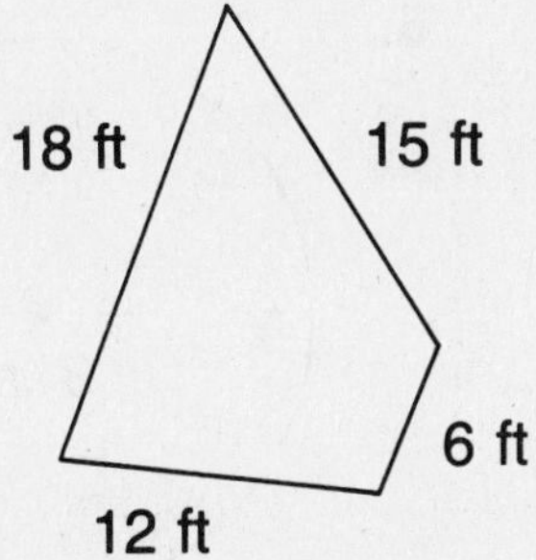

4.

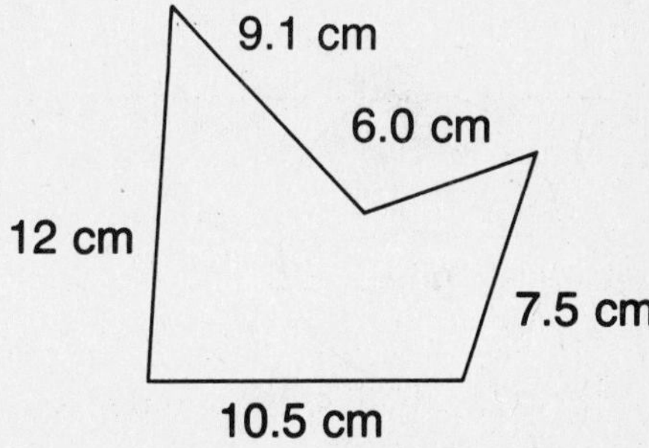

5. A triangle with sides 2.2 cm, 3.2 cm, and 2.8 cm long

6. A triangle with sides 22.4 m, 32.5 m, and 28.1 m long

7. A square with each side 61 ft long

8. A regular pentagon with each side 3.5 cm long

Critical Thinking The perimeter of a square is 280 inches. What is the length of each side?

Circumference

Find the circumference of each circle.
Use 3.14 for π.

1.

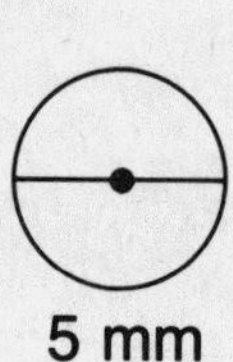

2.

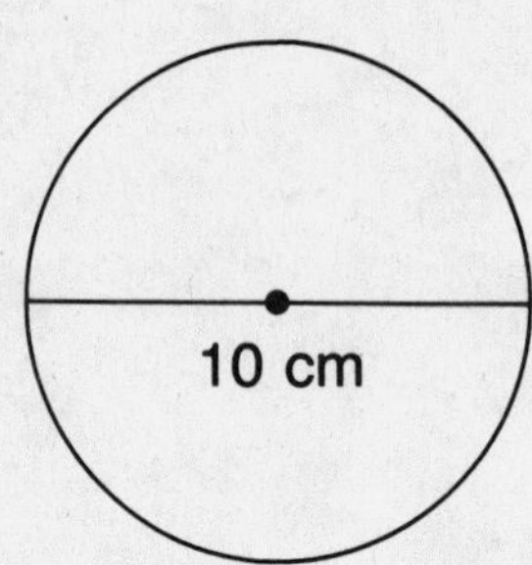

3.

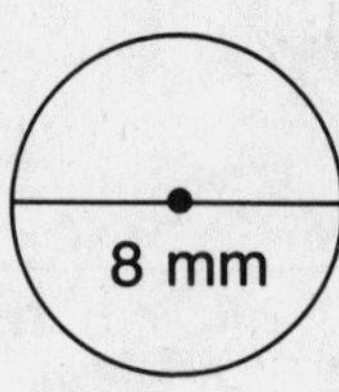

4.

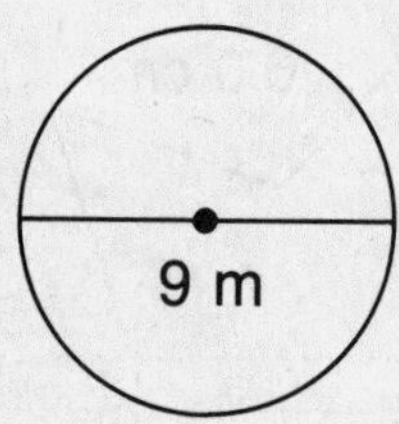

5.

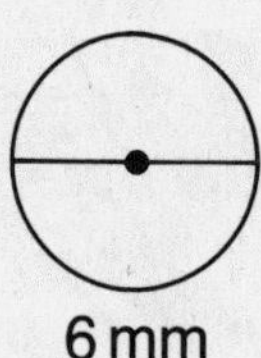

6.

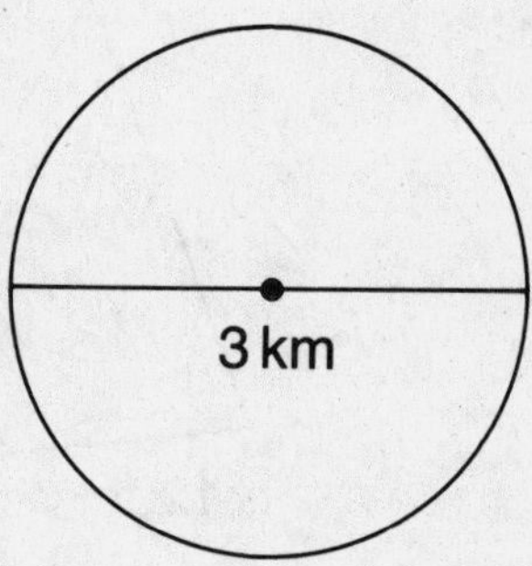

Find the circumference of a circle with the given diameter. Use 3.14 for π.

Diameter	**7.** 30 cm	**8.** 1.9 cm	**9.** 16 ft
Circumference			

Solve each problem. Use 3.14 for π.

10. A circular crater has a circumference of 43.96 m. Find its diameter. ________

11. A circular design has a circumference of 109.9 mm. Find the radius. ________

NAME

SHARPEN YOUR SKILLS

Make a Table

Make a table and look for a pattern to solve each problem.

1. Find the perimeter of a chain of 75 equilateral triangles. Each side is 3 cm long.

____

2. Find the perimeter of a chain of 60 hexagons. Each side is 4 in. long.

____

3. Find the perimeter of a chain of 50 octagons. Each side is 2 m long.

____

4. Find the perimeter of a chain of 50 pentagons. Each side is 1 ft long.

____

Use after pages 346–347.

NAME

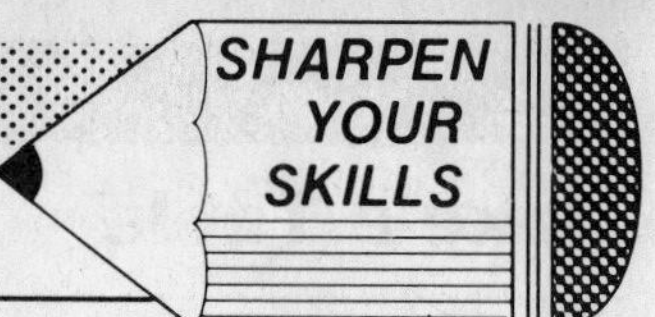

Area of Rectangles and Squares

Estimation Estimate the area of each figure. Then find each area. **Remember** that area is always expressed in square units.

1.

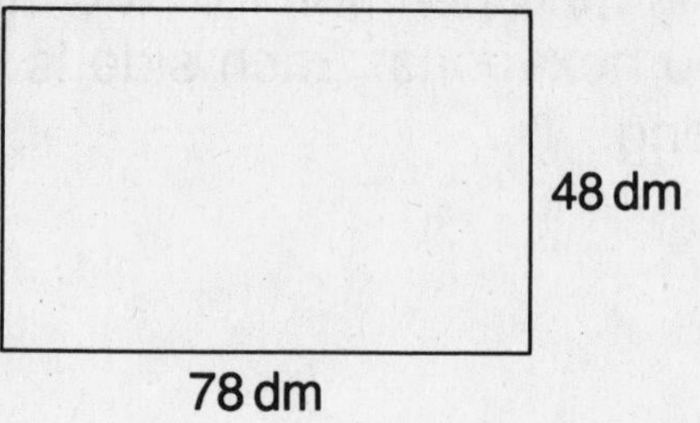

2.

3.

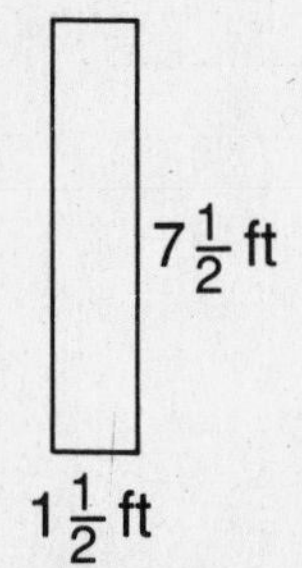

4.

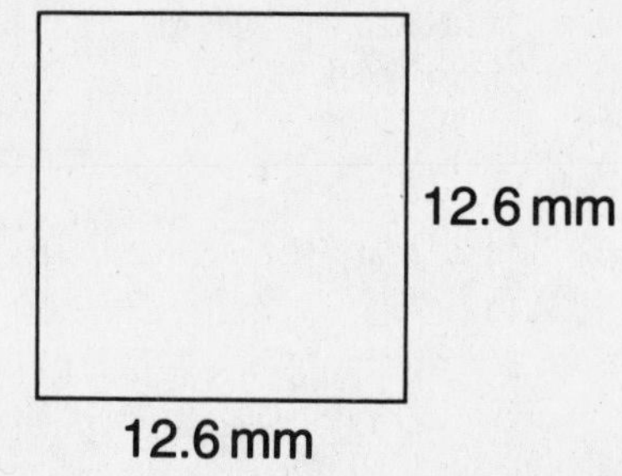

Find the area of each shaded region.

5.

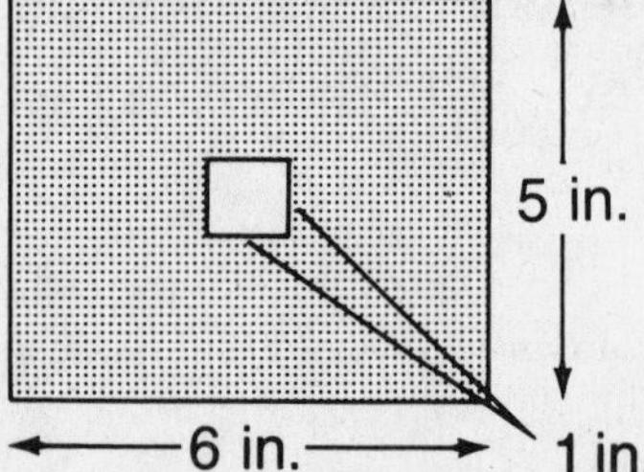

6.

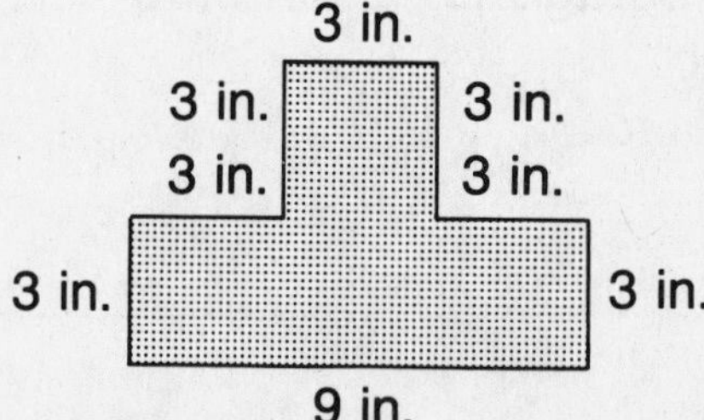

Solve each problem.

Hilda and Joe built rectangular sandcastles with the following measures. Find the area.

7. 1.8 cm by 2.2 cm

8. 5.5 cm by 8 cm

NAME

SHARPEN YOUR SKILLS

Area of Parallelograms and Triangles

Find the area of each figure. **Remember** to give your answer in square units.

1.

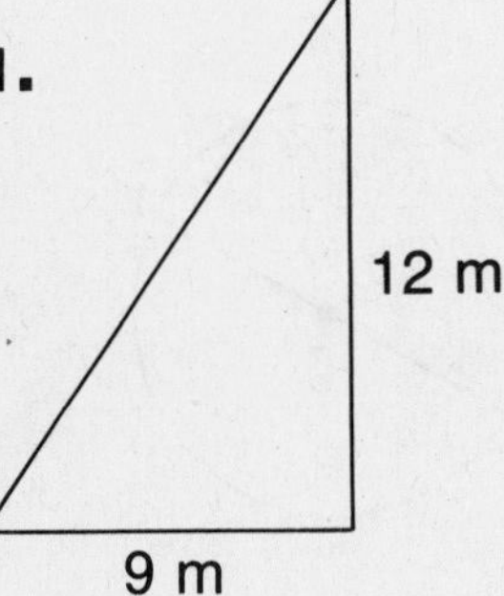

2.

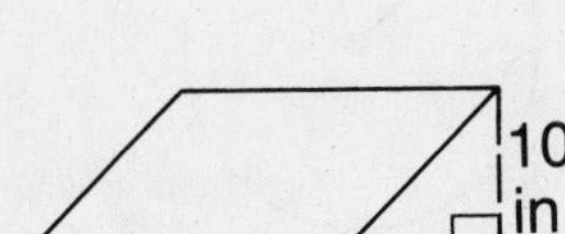

3.

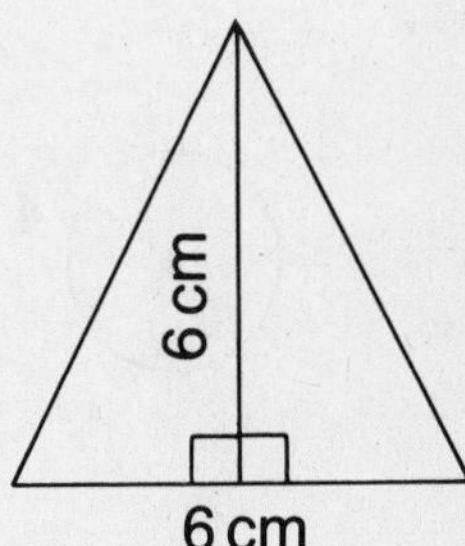

4.

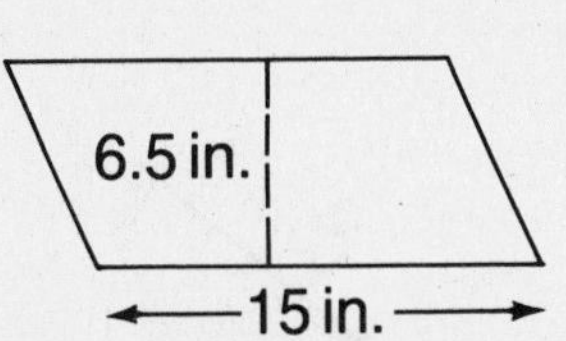

5.

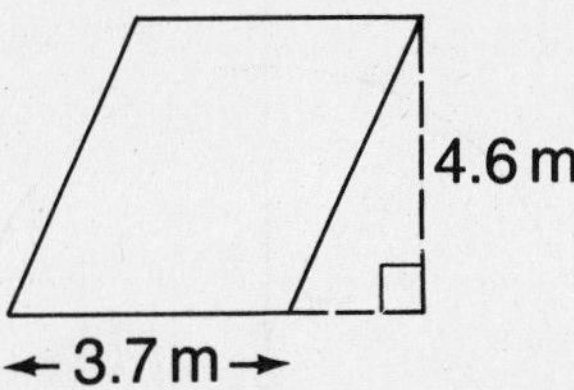

6.

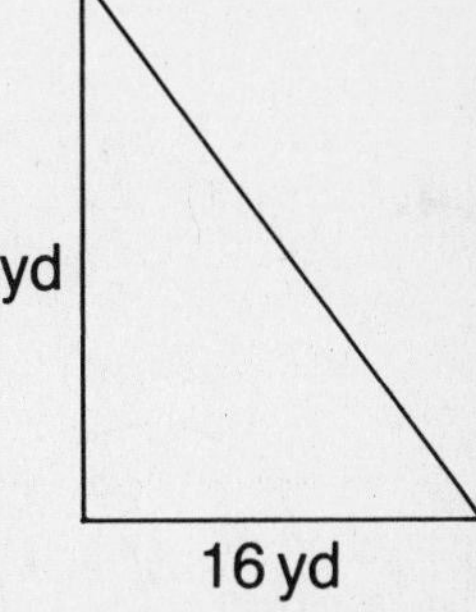

7. A parallelogram with base 5.6 mm and height 7.8 mm

8. A triangle with base 6.3 in. and height 12.7 in.

9.

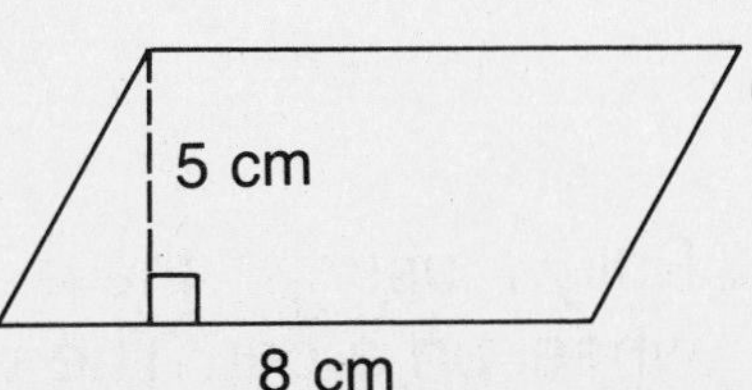

10.

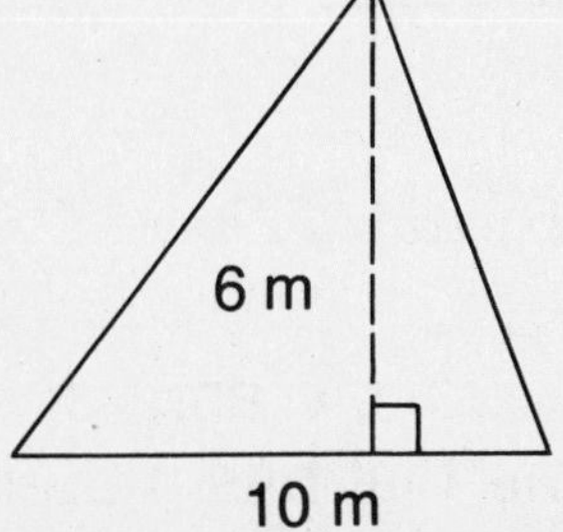

Use after pages 350–353.

NAME

SHARPEN YOUR SKILLS

Area of Circles

Estimation Estimate the area of each circle. Then find each area. **Remember** that area is measured in square units.

1.

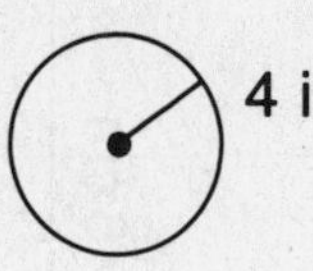

2.

3.

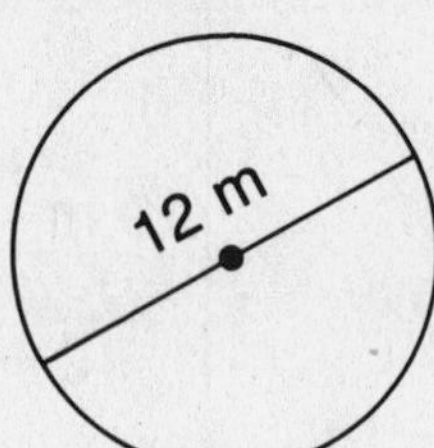

______ ______ ______

4.

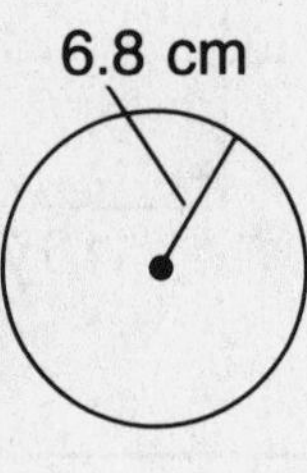

5.

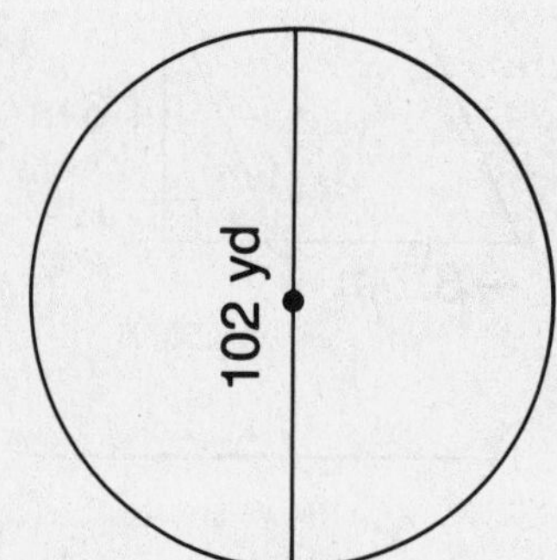

6.

______ ______ ______

7. Radius: 4.5 cm

8. Radius: 8 in.

9. Diameter: 6.5 m

______ ______ ______

Solve each problem.

10. Joann must find the area of a circular frame that has a 25-in. radius. What is the area?

______

11. Polly must find the area of a wheel on a car. The wheel has a 9-in. radius. What is the area?

______

NAME

SHARPEN YOUR SKILLS

Use a Formula

Choose a formula from the table and then solve each problem.

	Square	Rectangle	Triangle
Area	$A = s^2$	$A = \ell \times w$	$A = \frac{1}{2} \times b \times h$
Perimeter	$P = 4 \times s$	$P = 2 \times \ell + 2 \times w$	$P = a + b + c$

1. A hamster's cage takes up 126 square inches of floor space. If the length of the cage is 9 inches, what is the width?

2. A rectangular-shaped house is 36 feet wide and 66 feet long. What is its area? What is the perimeter?

3. The front of a doghouse is in the shape of a triangle. How high is the doghouse if the base of the front is 24 inches and the area is 432 square inches?

4. The O'Neils' living room is 22 feet by 15 feet. They want to put down a rug with an area of 350 square feet. Will the rug fit?

5. A square log cabin is 16 feet on each side. What is its area?

6. What is the perimeter of the log cabin in Exercise 5?

NAME

SHARPEN YOUR SKILLS

Surface Area of Prisms

Find the surface area of each prism. **Remember** to include the area of each face.

1.

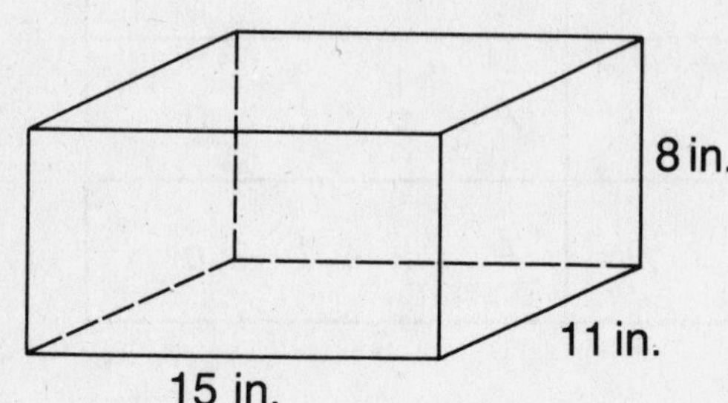

2.

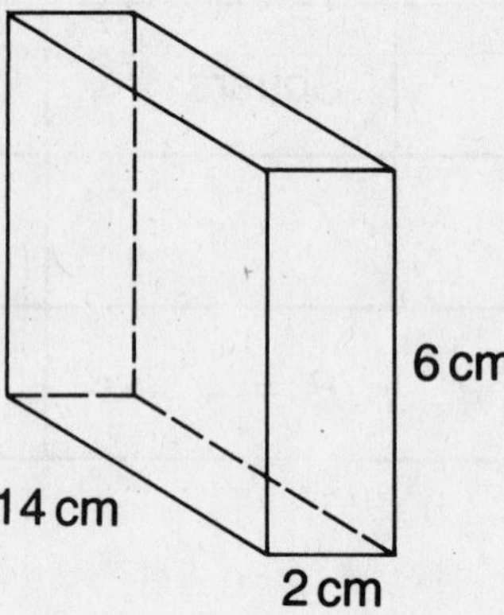

3.

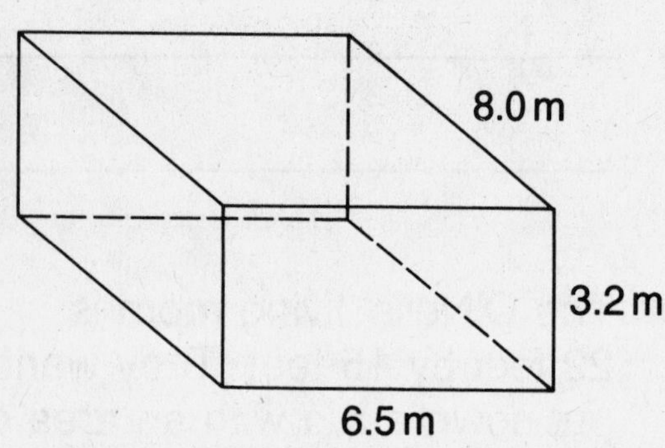

4.

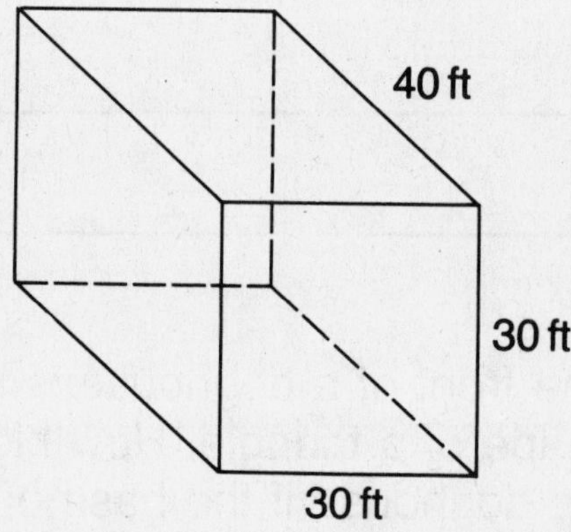

5.

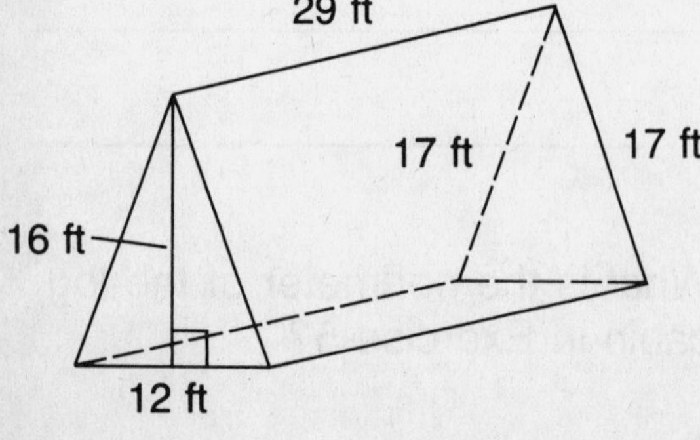

6.

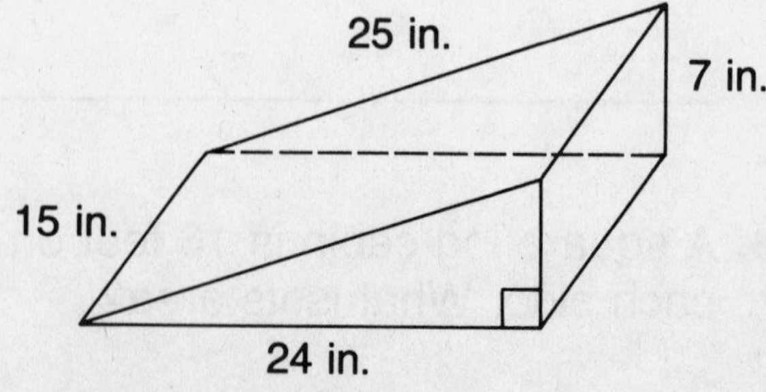

NAME

SHARPEN YOUR SKILLS

Volume of Prisms

Find the volume of each prism. **Remember** to use cubic units in your answer.

1.

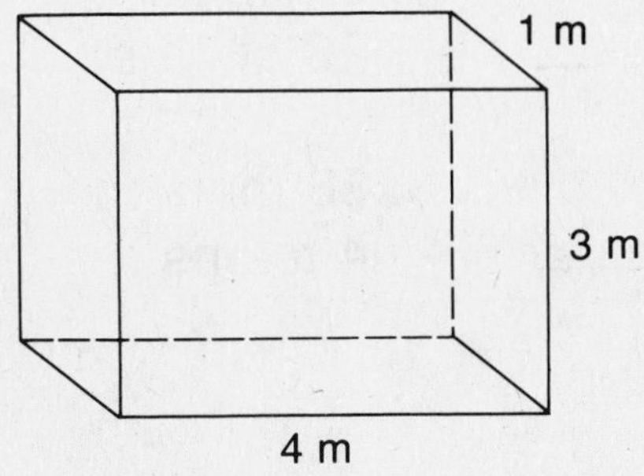

2.

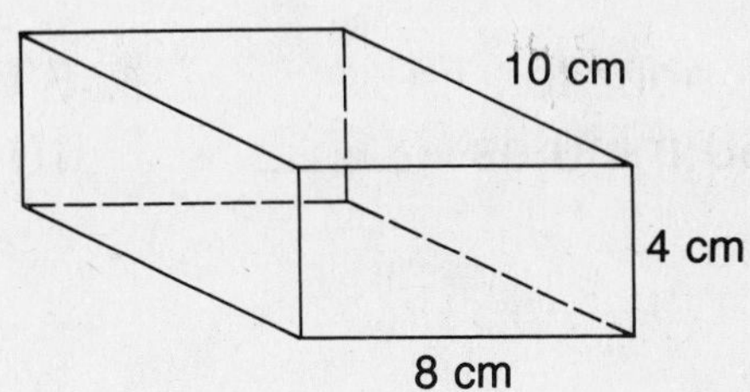

3.

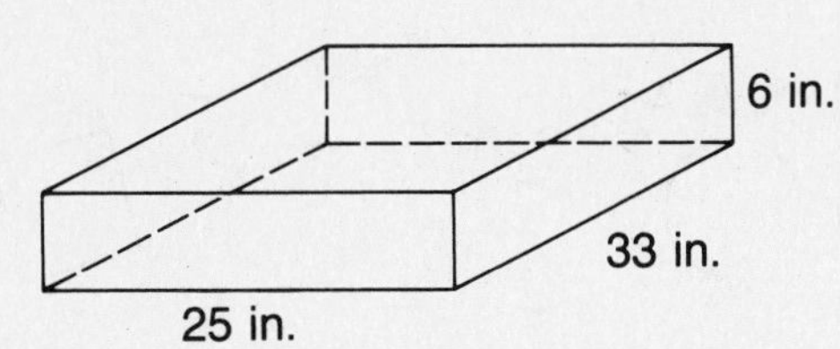

4.

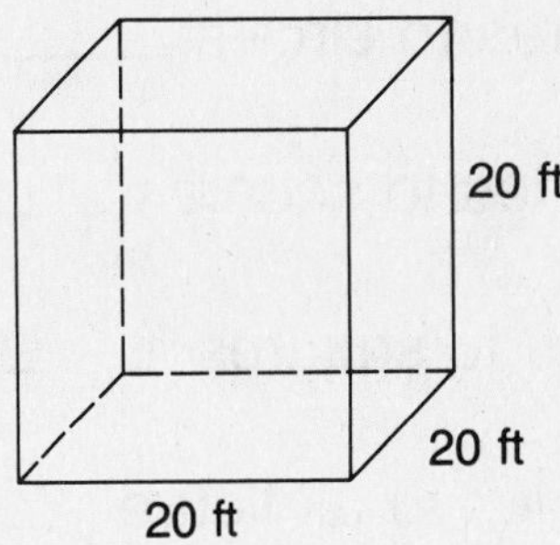

Find the volume of each rectangular prism.

	Length	Width	Height	Volume
5.	14 in.	6 in.	3 in.	
6.	2.8 mm	1.5 mm	0.3 mm	
7.	7.0 ft	6.9 ft	3.1 ft	

Solve the problem.

8. Oranges were shipped in rectangular boxes to a grocery store. Each box was 60 in. long, 40 in. wide, and 32 in. high. Find the volume of each box.

NAME

SHARPEN YOUR SKILLS

Ratios

Write a ratio for each situation.

1. 58 people to 10 tables ____
2. 65 girls on 7 teams ____
3. 8 hits for 20 at bats ____
4. 1 hour to 60 minutes ____
5. 6 wins in 10 games ____
6. 96 men on 4 teams ____

Use the picture. Write a ratio for

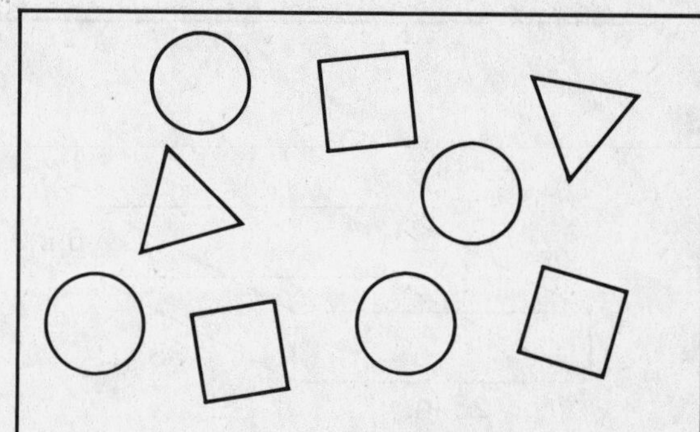

7. squares to circles ____
8. triangles to squares ____
9. circles to squares ____
10. triangles to all figures ____

Use the table to find each ratio.

Team	W	L
California	63	40
Oakland	62	42
Kansas City	57	47
Texas	56	47
Minnesota	51	53
Seattle	49	54
Chicago	44	60

11. California games won to games lost ____
12. Minnesota games won to games played ____
13. Oakland games lost to games played ____
14. Chicago games lost to games won ____
15. Texas games won to Seattle games won ____
16. Chicago games lost to games played ____
17. Texas games won to Oakland games won ____
18. Kansas City games won to games lost ____

NAME

SHARPEN YOUR SKILLS

Equal Ratios

Mental Math Complete each equation.

1. $\frac{5}{9}(\times \quad) = \frac{10}{18}$ **2.** $\frac{18}{21}(\div \quad) = \frac{6}{7}$ **3.** $\frac{75}{50}(\div \quad) = \frac{3}{2}$

Make a diagram of each ratio.

4. 3 cans for $7

5. 5 people per house

Find two ratios that are equal to the given ratio. In each exercise, use multiplication once and division once.

6. $\frac{4}{8}$ **7.** $\frac{40}{30}$ **8.** $\frac{25}{75}$

Complete each table to show equal ratios.

9.

inches	1	2	3	5	8
miles	25	50	75		

10.

ounces	64	32	16	8
pounds	4	2		

Solve each problem. Show your work.

11. On a state map, 5 miles are represented by 2 inches. Write a ratio and find how many miles one inch will equal.

12. A plane travels 1,500 miles in 2.5 hours. Write a ratio and find the plane's average speed per hour.

Use after pages 378–381.

NAME

SHARPEN YOUR SKILLS

Proportions

Do the ratios form a proportion?

Draw lines to connect the ratios that form proportions. You will find a path through the maze from START to FINISH.

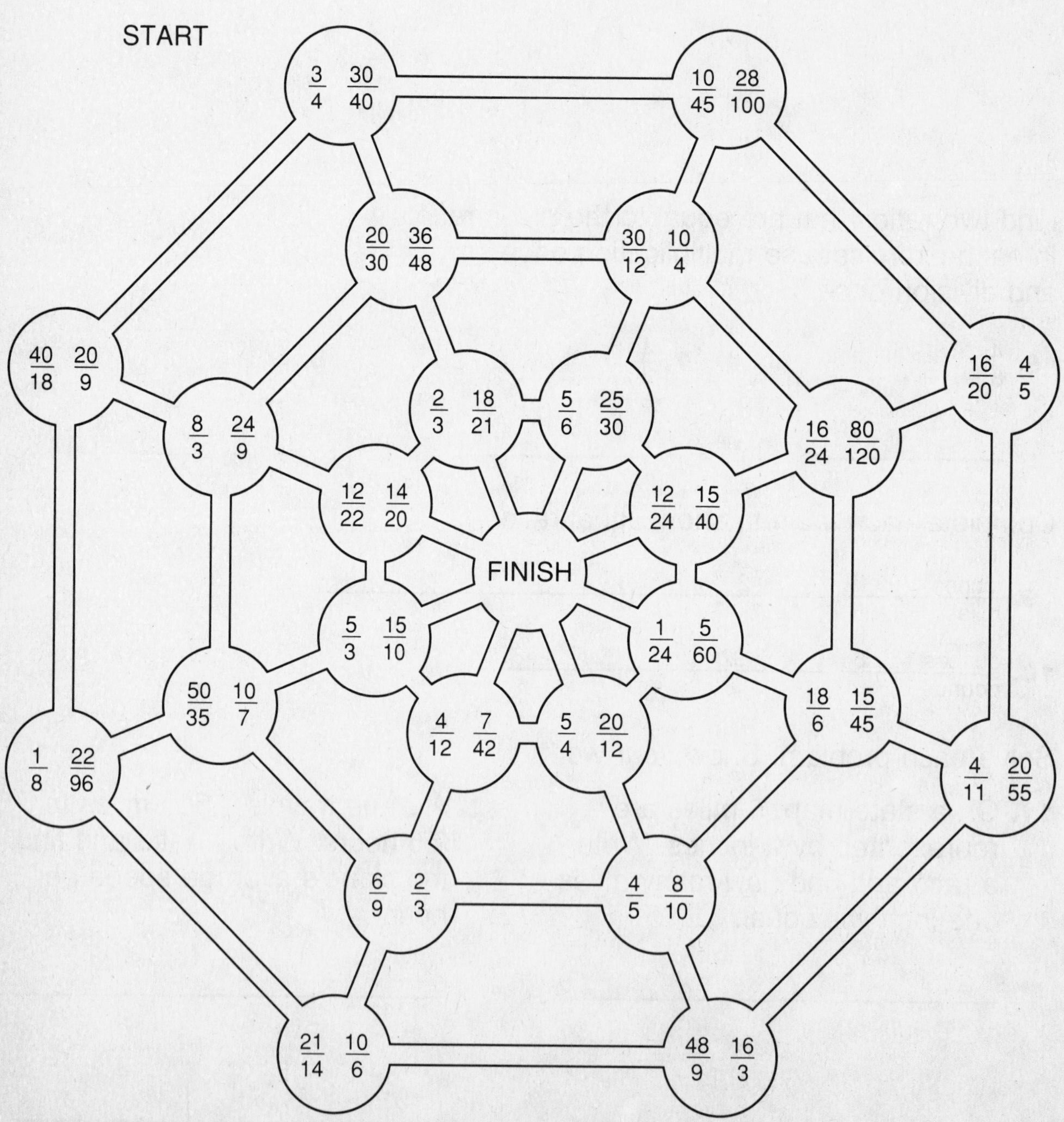

NAME

SHARPEN YOUR SKILLS

Solving Proportions

Solve each proportion. Double check your answers.

1. $\frac{2}{3} = \frac{n}{18}$ ______

2. $\frac{5}{3} = \frac{15}{n}$ ______

3. $\frac{n}{18} = \frac{3}{27}$ ______

4. $\frac{64}{n} = \frac{14}{7}$ ______

5. $\frac{9}{n} = \frac{12}{36}$ ______

6. $\frac{45}{18} = \frac{n}{6}$ ______

Use cross products to solve each problem.
Estimate first to be sure your answer is reasonable.

7. $\frac{n}{45} = \frac{4}{18}$ ______

8. $\frac{14}{10} = \frac{63}{n}$ ______

9. $\frac{n}{35} = \frac{9}{15}$ ______

In each exercise, decide whether $t = 39$ is a reasonable answer. Explain.

10. $\frac{55}{t} = \frac{600}{450}$ ______

11. $\frac{t}{55} = \frac{600}{450}$ ______

12. $\frac{55}{600} = \frac{t}{450}$ ______

Solve.

13. If 7 ounces of oil are mixed with 3 ounces of vinegar, how many ounces of oil will be mixed with 10 ounces of vinegar? ______

14. The cost to enlarge 3 pictures is $2.50. At this price, how much would the cost be to enlarge 36 pictures? ______

NAME

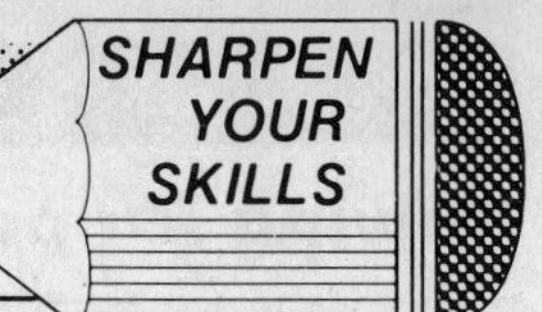

Write an Equation

1. Complete the set of equal rates for a plane traveling 600 miles an hour. (Hint: 1 mile = 5,280 feet.)

$$\frac{600 \text{ mi}}{1 \text{ hr}} = \frac{\_\_\_\_ \text{ mi}}{60 \text{ min}} = \frac{\_\_\_\_ \text{ mi}}{1 \text{ min}} = \frac{\_\_\_\_ \text{ ft}}{1 \text{ min}} = \frac{\_\_\_\_ \text{ ft}}{60 \text{ sec}} = \frac{\_\_\_\_ \text{ ft}}{1 \text{ sec}}$$

For each of the following, write the correct equation and then solve it.

2. If you exercise 2 hours a day, how many hours will you spend exercising in a year?

____

3. If workers can paint a 1-story house in 8 hours, how long will it take them to paint two 3-story houses?

____

4. Biking at a rate of 25 miles in 2 hours, how far could you bike in 5 hours?

____

5. If a car travels 100 miles in 3 hours, about how long will it take to travel 160 miles?

____

6. Some birds eat twice their own weight in a day. At that rate, how much would a 120-pound boy eat in a day?

____

7. A man weighing 150 pounds on earth weighs 25 pounds on the moon. What will be the moon weight of a woman who weighs 120 pounds on earth?

____

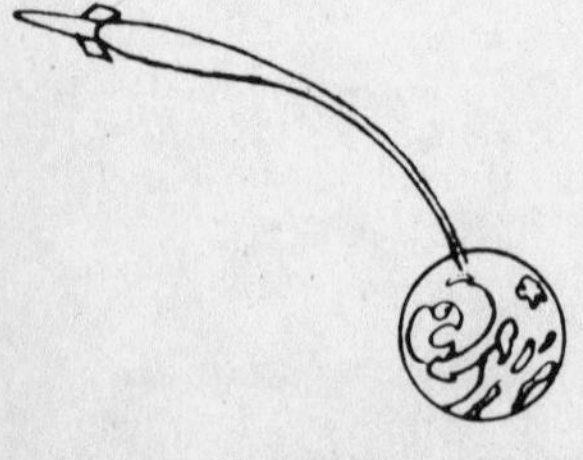

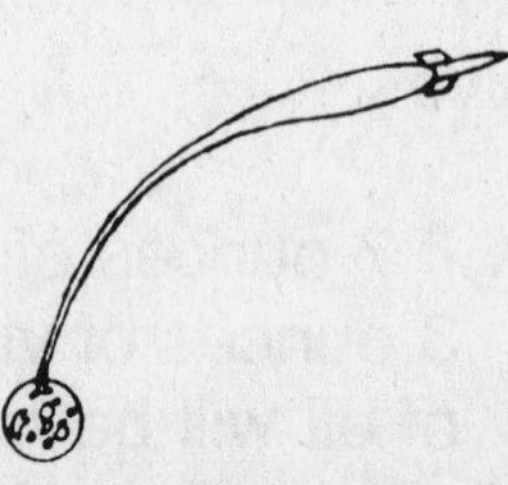

Critical Thinking Read Exercise 7 again. Would it take more power or less power to lift a rocket from the moon than from the earth?

____

NAME

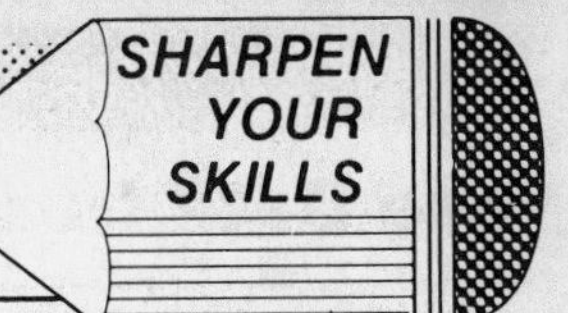

Similar Figures

1. Name the corresponding sides in these similar triangles.

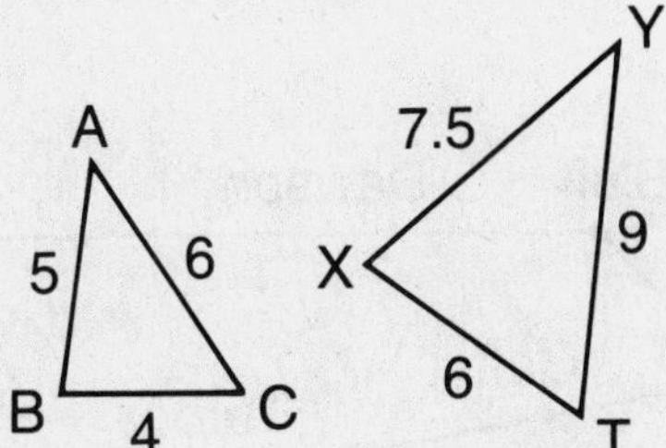

2. Prove the two rectangles are not similar.

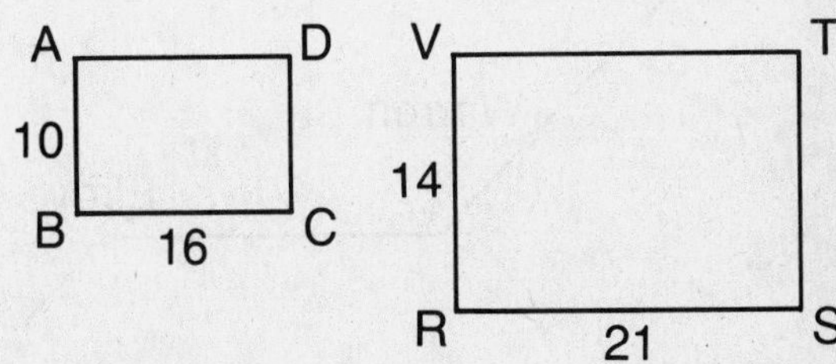

For each pair of similar figures, find *n*.

3.

8
n
12
24

4.

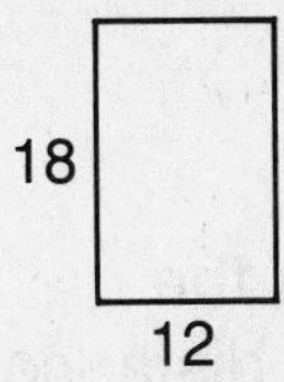

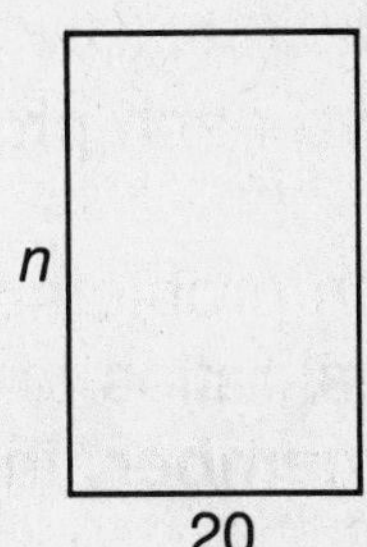

Solve each problem.

5. The triangles formed by the boy and his shadow and the pole and its shadow are similar. Find the height of the pole.

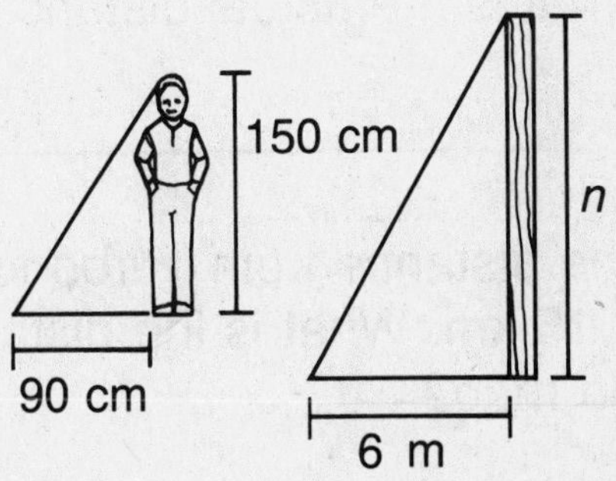

6. A picture and its album form similar rectangles. How wide is the album?

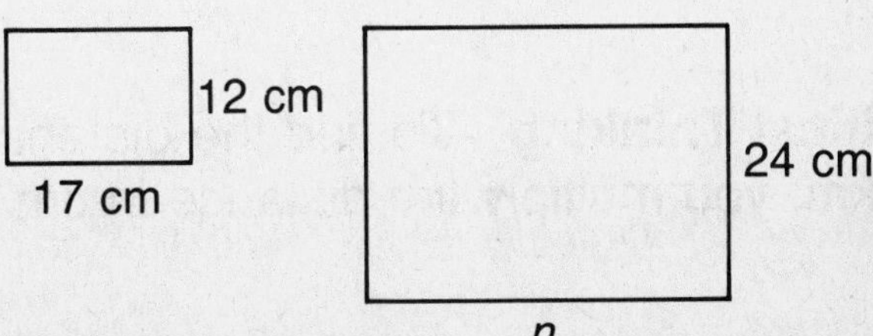

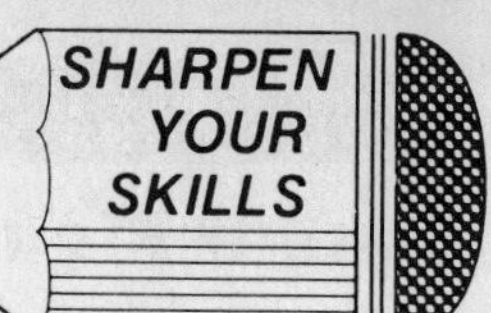

Use Data from a Diagram

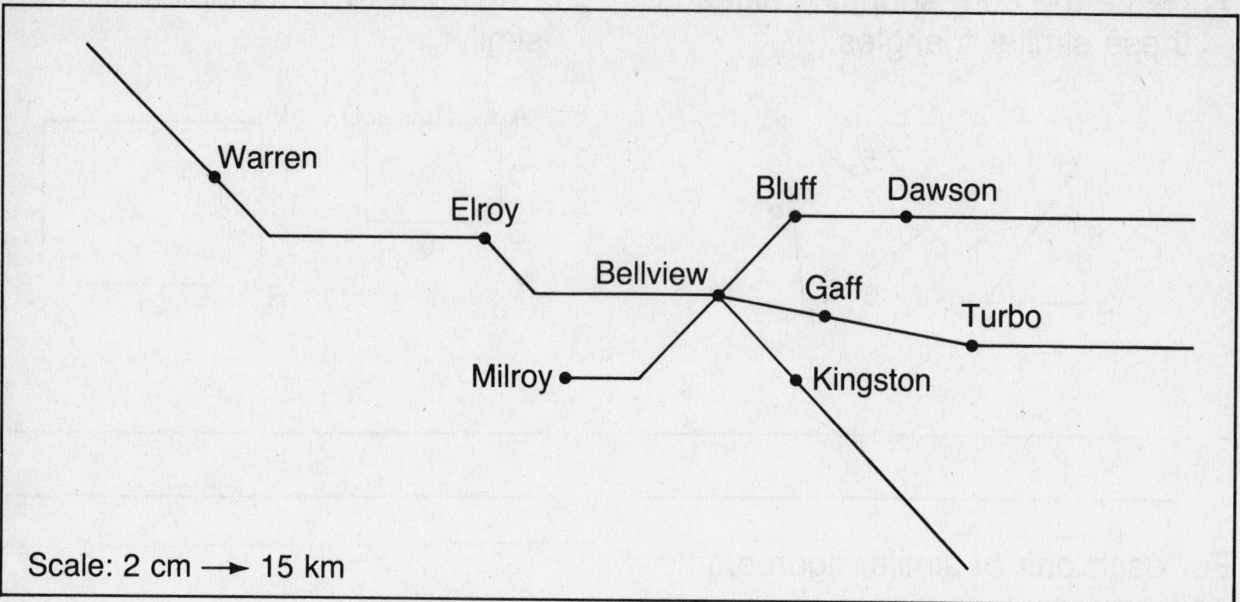

Solve each problem.

Each problem refers to the map above. Use equal ratios to find the distances. **Remember,** the scale is 2 cm to 15 km.

1. The distance from Kingston to Bellview on the map is 1.5 cm. What is the actual distance?

____

2. Milroy is 18.75 km from Bellview. What is the distance on the map?

____

3. The distance from Turbo to Gaff is 15 km. What is the distance on the map?

____

4. The distance from Warren to Elroy on the map is 4.2 cm. What is the actual distance?

____

Critical Thinking To find the distance between cities in km, you multiply the distance in cm by what factor?

____

NAME

SHARPEN YOUR SKILLS

Percents as Ratios

Mental Math Express each ratio as a percent.

1. $\frac{71}{100}$ ________ E **2.** $\frac{99}{100}$ ________ B **3.** $\frac{6}{100}$ ________ N

Write each percent as a ratio.

4. 27% ________ E **5.** 62% ________ L **6.** 75% ________ C

7. 2% ________ T **8.** 41% ________ T **9.** 90% ________ I

10. 15% ________ N **11.** 9% ________ C **12.** 50% ________ A

Write each ratio as a percent.

13. $\frac{7}{10}$ ________ E **14.** $\frac{1}{5}$ ________ O **15.** $\frac{7}{20}$ ________ A

16. $\frac{1}{50}$ ________ I **17.** $\frac{4}{5}$ ________ E **18.** $\frac{3}{100}$ ________ L

19. $\frac{9}{10}$ ________ N **20.** $\frac{9}{25}$ ________ R **21.** $\frac{13}{20}$ ________ N

Fill in the letters that match the answers below.

Wait awhile for this party.

___	___	___	___	___	___	___	___	___	___
$\frac{75}{100}$	71%	90%	$\frac{41}{100}$	80%	6%	65%	$\frac{90}{100}$	35%	$\frac{62}{100}$

___	___	___	___	___	___	___	___	___	___	___
$\frac{9}{100}$	$\frac{27}{100}$	3%	70%	99%	36%	$\frac{50}{100}$	$\frac{2}{100}$	2%	20%	$\frac{15}{100}$

SHARPEN YOUR SKILLS

Collecting Data

Ask 25 of your classmates which of the three following activities they spend the most time on.

1. (A) watching TV
2. (B) listening to the radio
3. (C) reading

Tally Sheet		
1.	2.	3.

Record your answers on the tally sheet.

Using the collected data, set up proportions to find the answers to exercises 4, 5, 6, and 7.

4. What percent watch TV? ______

5. What percent listen to the radio? ______

6. What percent read? ______

7. Was any activity named by more than 50% of the students? ______

Set up a proportion to find the answers to exercises 8 and 9.

8. Select 4 school subjects and ask 10 classmates to select the one that they like best. ______

9. Find the percent of students who selected each subject. ______

Explain.

10. If 35% of the people in your class read, then how many individual people does this represent? ______

11. If 20% of the people in your class watch television, then how many individual people does this represent? ______

NAME

SHARPEN YOUR SKILLS

Percents and Decimals

Write each percent as a decimal.

1. 17% ____________ **2.** 82% ____________ **3.** 90% ____________

4. 1% ____________ **5.** 34% ____________ **6.** 6% ____________

7. 1.5% ____________ **8.** 56% ____________ **9.** 75% ____________

10. 22.8% ____________ **11.** 30% ____________ **12.** $66\frac{2}{3}$% ____________

Write each decimal as a percent.

13. 0.26 ____________ **14.** 0.08 ____________ **15.** 0.19 ____________

16. 0.39 ____________ **17.** 0.77 ____________ **18.** 0.2 ____________

19. 0.6 ____________ **20.** 0.238 ____________ **21.** 0.815 ____________

22. 0.02 ____________ **23.** 0.075 ____________ **24.** $0.33\frac{1}{3}$ ____________

Solve each problem.

25. A message had a total of 200 letters, of which 34% were As. How many As were in the message? ____________

26. Of the 300 students in the Computer Club, 150 are sixth graders. What percent are sixth graders? ____________

27. Of the 300 students in the Computer Club, 15 percent are seventh graders. How many club members are seventh graders? ____________

28. The Computer Club collected $300 in dues. They decided to spend 28% on a club party. How much will be spent on their party? ____________

Use after pages 416–417.

NAME

SHARPEN YOUR SKILLS

Percents and Fractions

Write each percent as a fraction in lowest terms.

1. 37% ________ **2.** 83% ________ **3.** 7% ________

4. 16% ________ **5.** 24% ________ **6.** 32% ________

7. 54% ________ **8.** 45% ________ **9.** 2% ________

When do spacemen eat lunch?

To find out, write each fraction as a percent. Then cross out the box containing each answer. Write the remaining letters in order on the blanks below the chart.

10. $\frac{29}{100}$ ________ **11.** $\frac{17}{100}$ ________ **12.** $\frac{9}{100}$ ________

13. $\frac{7}{10}$ ________ **14.** $\frac{3}{5}$ ________ **15.** $\frac{1}{2}$ ________

16. $\frac{1}{5}$ ________ **17.** $\frac{1}{25}$ ________ **18.** $\frac{6}{25}$ ________

19. $\frac{17}{50}$ ________ **20.** $\frac{13}{25}$ ________ **21.** $\frac{3}{20}$ ________

A 10%	D 20%	T 5%	L 59%	S 9%	J 34%	A 12%	P 60%	W 24%	U 35%	N 40%	Z 17%
F 70%	C 19%	G 50%	H 43%	T 75%	Q 4%	V 52%	I 22%	M 62%	K 29%	J 15%	E 18%

____ ____   ____ ____ ____ ____ ____ ____   ____ ____ ____ ____

NAME

SHARPEN YOUR SKILLS

Percents, Decimals, and Fractions

Mixed Practice Complete the tables with equivalent percents, decimals, and fractions.

Fraction	Decimal	Percent
$\frac{1}{50}$	**1.** ____ I	**2.** ____ Y
3. ____ N	**4.** ____ E	3%
5. ____ N	0.12	**6.** ____ E
$\frac{3}{8}$	**7.** ____ E	**8.** ____ E
9. ____ C	0.35	35%

Fraction	Decimal	Percent
10. ____ R	0.45	**11.** ____ N
12. ____ P	**13.** ____ T	50%
$\frac{18}{25}$	**14.** ____ T	**15.** ____ N
16. ____ I	0.90	90%
17. ____ N	1.0	100%

Match each letter to its answer on the blanks below.

This means "Almost Perfect."

____ ____ ____ ____ ____ ____ — ____ ____ ____ ____

1 0.02 $\frac{3}{25}$ 37.5% 0.50 2% 45% $\frac{9}{10}$ $\frac{3}{100}$ 0.375

____ ____ ____ ____ ____ ____ ____

$\frac{1}{2}$ 12% $\frac{9}{20}$ $\frac{7}{20}$ 0.03 72% 0.72

Solve the problem.

18. At Central Middle School, $\frac{1}{3}$ of the students are in sixth grade, 35% are in seventh grade and the rest are in eighth grade. Which grade has the most students? Which has the least?

____

SHARPEN YOUR SKILLS

Using a Fraction or a Decimal to Find a Percent of a Number

Find the percent of each number to complete the cross-number puzzle below. Each decimal point has its own box.

Across

1. 20% of 532

4. 50% of 1,600

5. 25% of 40

6. 3% of 239

9. 30% of 197

12. What number is 6% of 525?

13. What number is 4% of 357?

15. 80% of 1,200

16. 75% of 200

Down

1. 2% of 64

2. 75% of 625

3. 23% of 234

5. 75% of 14

7. 85% of 84

8. What number is $33\frac{1}{3}$% of 2,430?

10. What number is 90% of 1,000?

11. 10% of 125

14. 4% of 2,225

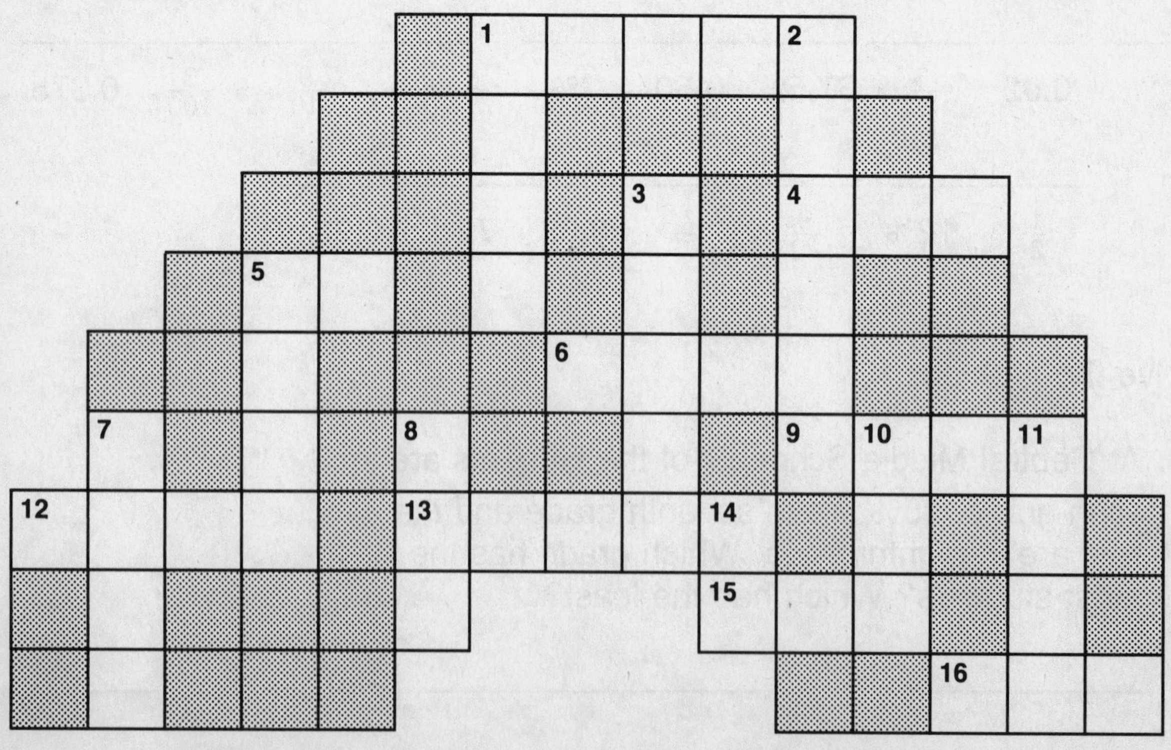

NAME

SHARPEN YOUR SKILLS

Mental Math: Percents

Use mental math to find each answer.

1. 50% of 10 ______

2. 10% of 70 ______

3. 75% of 8 ______

4. 20% of 90 ______

5. 80% of 65 ______

6. 60% of 20 ______

7. 25% of 200 ______

8. 40% of 50 ______

9. $66\frac{2}{3}$% of 36 ______

10. $33\frac{1}{3}$% of 72 ______

11. 25% of 36 ______

12. 50% of 40 ______

13. 12% of 50 ______

14. 30% of 110 ______

15. 65% of 100 ______

16. 90% of 300 ______

Solve each problem.

17. Grapes are about 77% water. What is the weight of the water in 10 pounds of grapes? ______

18. Watermelon is about 95% water. What is the weight of the water in a 20-pound watermelon? ______

19. About 12 million tons of oranges are harvested in the United States each year. About 75% of the oranges are processed for juice. How many tons of oranges are made into juice? ______

Use after pages 428–429.

NAME

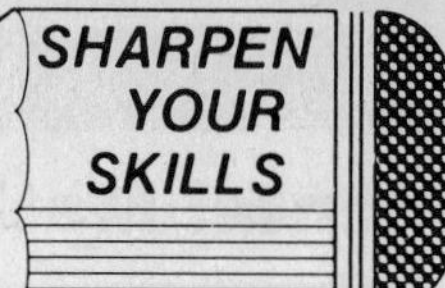

Estimating with Percents

Estimate to choose the most sensible answer.

1. 53% of 788

a. 418 **b.** 704 **c.** 230

2. 74% of 400

a. 100 **b.** 204 **c.** 296

3. 11% of 2,984

a. 32 **b.** 328 **c.** 2,685

4. 66% of 600

a. 300 **b.** 396 **c.** 496

Estimate. Tell if your answer is greater or less than the exact answer.

5. 19% of 500

6. 91% of 1,000

7. 50% of 813

8. $33\frac{1}{3}$% of 289

9. 78% of 250

10. 25% of 390

Critical Thinking For each situation tell whether you would want an exact answer, an estimate higher than the answer, or an estimate lower than the exact answer.

11. Total cost of articles as you shop ______

12. Amount of gas left in the tank of your car ______

13. Cost of merchandise when you pay cashier ______

Use after pages 430–431.

NAME

SHARPEN YOUR SKILLS

Multiple-Step Problems

Find the total price of each item including 5% sales tax.

1. Tennis shoes \$18.95

2. Soccer ball \$15.95

3. Golf ball \$0.95

4. Bowling shoes \$21.95

These items have gone on sale for 30% off the original price. What is the sale price?

5. Football \$14.95

6. Bowling shoes \$24.98

Solve each problem.

7. José has \$10.00. Can he buy a baseball bat that costs \$8.95 plus 6% tax? What is the final cost?

8. Sarah has \$30.00. Can she buy a fishing rod that costs \$28.95 plus 5% sales tax? What is the final cost?

Solve the problem.

9. You can buy a tent for \$1,000 in one state. In another state the price is 10% less, but there is a 10% tax. Which is the better buy?

Use after pages 432–433.

NAME

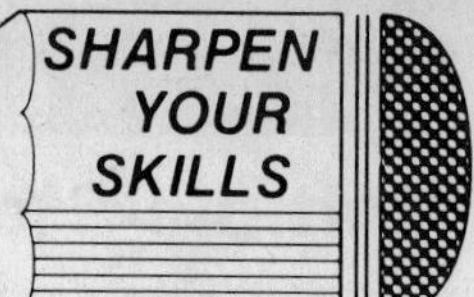

Find What Percent One Number Is of Another

Find each answer. **Remember** to express your answer as a percent.

1. 4 is what percent of 20? ______

2. 14 is what percent of 40? ______

3. 12 is what percent of 30? ______

4. 36 is what percent of 80? ______

5. What percent of 60 is 15? ______

6. What percent of 25 is 17? ______

7. What percent of 55 is 44? ______

8. What percent of 75 is 54? ______

9. Find what percent 31 is of 50. ______

10. Find what percent 34 is of 85. ______

Solve each problem.

A baseball team scored 25 runs. What percent of the runs did these players score?

11. James, 1 run ______

12. Joe, 6 runs ______

13. Milow, 4 runs ______

14. Robin, 5 runs ______

15. Carol, 3 runs ______

16. Clifton, 2 runs ______

NAME

SHARPEN YOUR SKILLS

Use Data from a Graph

The circle graph shows what percent each given music category is of the Good Sound Music Store's total sales.

The owners of the store are about to spend $1,400 on new tapes and records.

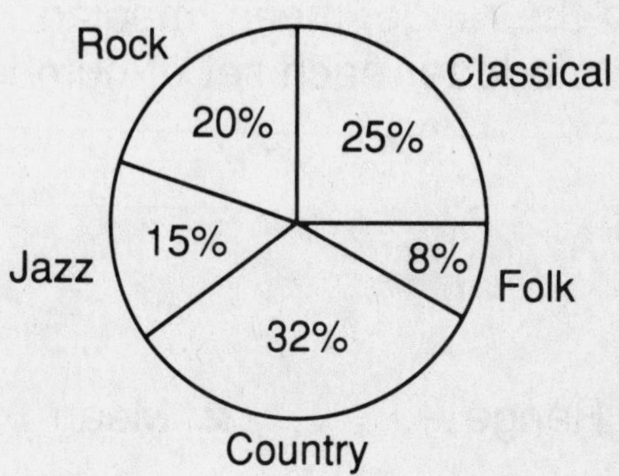

1. How much should they spend on rock?

2. How much should they spend on classical?

3. How much should they spend on folk music?

4. Which two categories account for just over half of the sales?

5. One day's sales were $198.71. Estimate how much of that was in classical music.

6. Estimate how much of that day's sales was in folk music.

7. Which category accounts for about one-third of the sales?

8. Which category brings in about one dollar out of five?

Critical Thinking Although classical music accounts for 25% of sales, only about 15% of the tapes, records, and disks are classical. Explain.

NAME

SHARPEN YOUR SKILLS

Range, Mean, Median, and Mode

Find the range, mean, median, and mode for each set of numbers.

Set A: 14 16 21 22 13 22 25

1. Range ______ **2.** Mean ______ **3.** Median ______ **4.** Mode ______

Set B: 34 43 44 55 44 56 32

5. Range ______ **6.** Mean ______ **7.** Median ______ **8.** Mode ______

Set C: 56 57 57 60 61 59 58 60 52 60 58

9. Range ______ **10.** Mean ______ **11.** Median ______ **12.** Mode ______

Find the missing numbers.

13. 27, 29, ______, 31, ______

Clues: mean = 30, range = 6

14. 15, ______, ______, 23, 27

Clues: mean = 20, mode = 15

NAME

SHARPEN YOUR SKILLS

Give Sensible Answers

Which average does each of the following describe—mean, median, or mode?

1. The average score on a math test was 79, but no one actually received that score.

____

2. More students received a score of 82 than any other score.

____

3. The school nurse weighed 18 students. Then she listed their weights in order. The average of the ninth and tenth weights was 99 pounds.

____

4. The nurse found that the average of all 18 weights was 97 pounds.

____

5. Of 9 students who took a history test, 5 received a score of 94.

____

6. A school survey of 35 sixth-grade students showed that the students spent an average homework time of 45 minutes per subject.

____

7. Of the 35 sixth graders surveyed, 12 students spent 43 minutes per subject.

____

8. In the homework survey, the eighteenth time listed was 44 minutes.

____

NAME

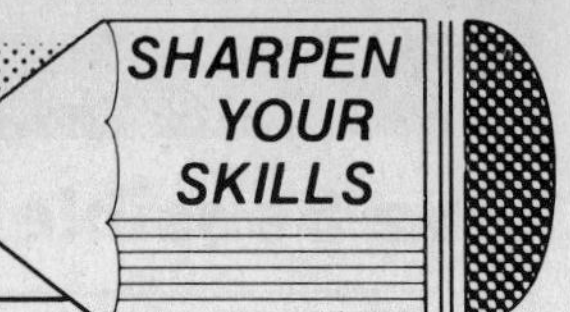

Statistical Graphs

Commercial Fishing Statistics for One Year

Country	
Japan	
Soviet Union	
China	
Norway	Each means 1,000,000 fish.
United States	

Percentage of Total Fish Caught by Country

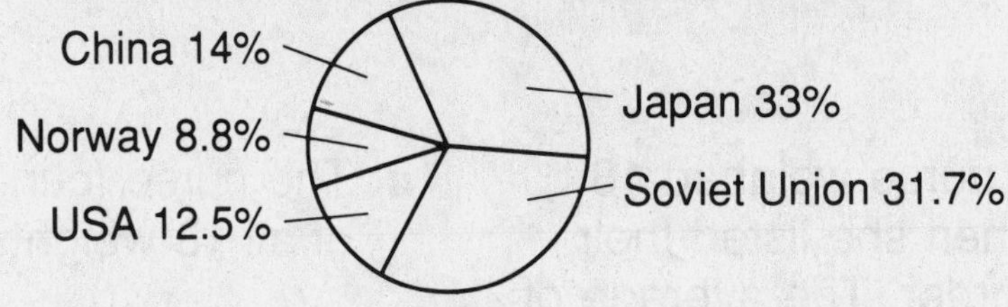

Use the appropriate graph to answer each question.

1. About how many fish were caught in the Soviet Union?

____

2. What percentage of the total fish caught were caught in Norway?

____

3. Which country caught 14% of the total amount of fish caught?

____

4. About how many fish were caught in the United States?

____

5. What was the total amount of fish caught by Norway?

____

6. What was the total percentage of fish caught by Japan and the Soviet Union?

____

7. Which country caught about 4,000,000 fish?

____

8. Which country caught about 9,500,000 fish?

____

NAME

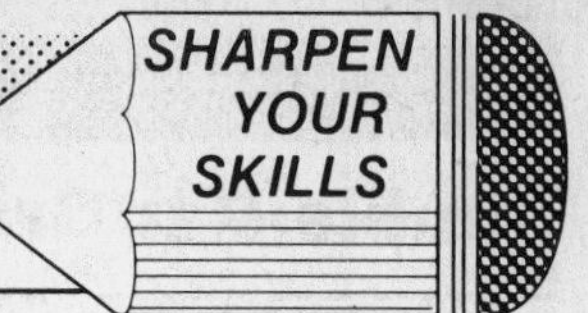

Interpreting Graphs

Write whether you would use a broken-line graph or a bar graph to show the following data.

1. The number of people who attended the Rose Bowl each year from 1947-1965.

____

2. The attendance on the same day for 6 different football games.

____

3. The number of games won by each team in the Pacific-10 conference for the year 1987.

____

4. The total number of people who attended Pacific-10 conference games each year from 1986-1988.

____

For each statement, draw and label the numerical scale you would use to graph the information.

Remember to use a zig-zag to indicate a broken scale.

5. The daily water use in the United States has risen from 200 billion gallons in 1950 to 450 billion gallons in 1980.

6. The weight of a student changed from 97 to 125 pounds between 1986 and 1989.

NAME ____________________

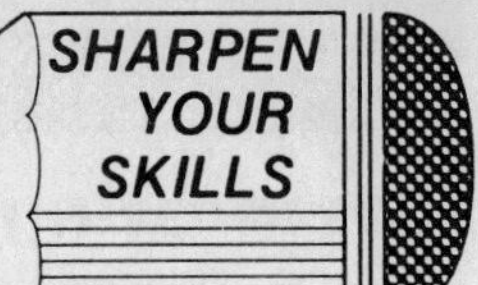

Double-Bar Graphs

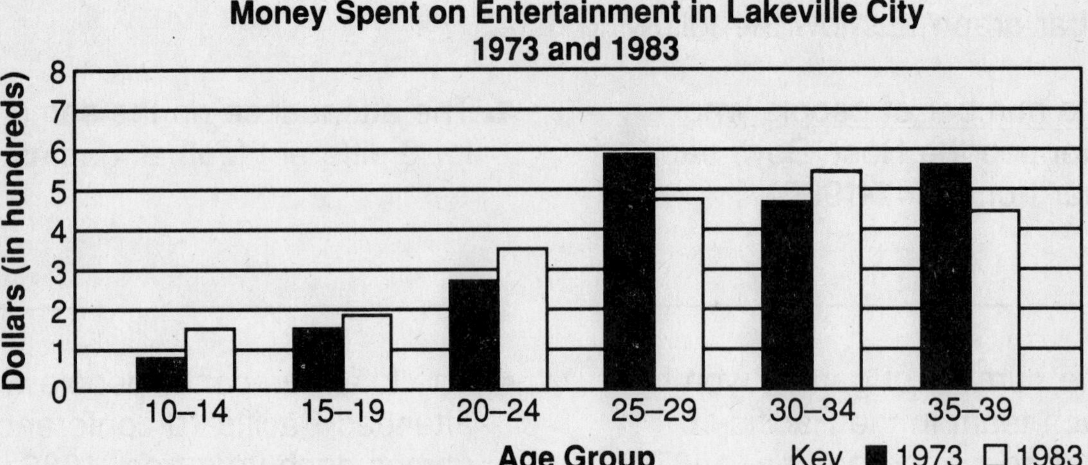

Use the graph to answer the questions.

1. Which two age groups spent the most money in 1983?

____

2. Which age groups spent less than $200 in 1983?

____

3. For which age groups was there a decrease in spending between 1973 and 1983?

____

4. Which age group spent the most money in either year? Which year was that?

____

5. Which group spent the least money in 1973?

____

6. Which age groups spent over $500 and in what years?

____

7. About how much money did the 30-34 year age group spend in 1983?

____

8. About how much did the 25-29 year age group spend in 1973 and 1983 combined?

____

NAME

SHARPEN YOUR SKILLS

Circle Graphs

Last year 650 students attended the Lane School Book Fair. The circle graph shows which kinds of books they bought.

How many students bought

1. mystery books? ________________

2. sports books? ________________

3. animal books? ________________

4. puzzle books? ________________

5. adventure books? ________________

Mystery 40%
Puzzle 10%
Animal 8%
Sports 20%
Adventure 22%

A survey questioned 1,200 12-year-olds about their favorite activities. The circle graph shows the responses.

How many students favored

6. roller skating? ________________

7. model building? ________________

8. record collecting? ________________

9. bicycle riding? ________________

10. reading?

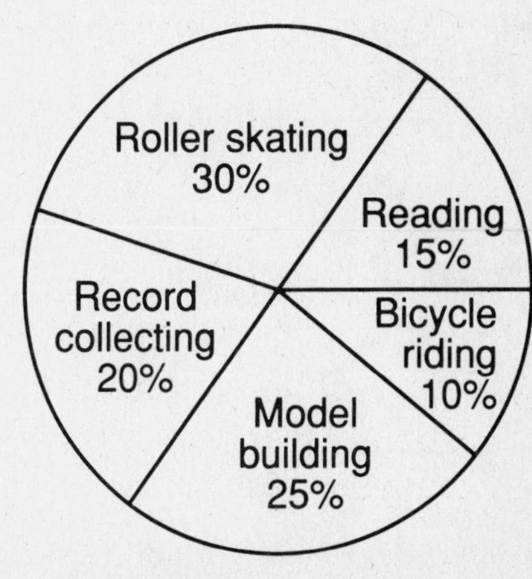

NAME

SHARPEN YOUR SKILLS

Make a Graph

Decide what type of graph will best show each type of data. Then draw the graph. **Remember** to use a title and label the scale.

Hint: **Bar graphs** are best for comparing data. **Circle graphs** are best for showing parts of a whole. **Line graphs** are best for showing data over a period of time.

1. Distance flown at 250 miles per hour between the hours of 9 A.M. and 1 P.M.

2. Distances flown in one day by four airplanes: 2,250 mi, 2,543 mi, 2,763 mi, and 2,102 mi.

3. Miles flown by one airplane each day of a week.

Mon.	Tues.	Wed.	Thurs.	Fri.
2,300	2,200	2,500	2,000	2,600

4. Food preferences of passengers on transcontinental flights.

Preferences

Beef	Chicken	Fish	No Meat	Kosher	No Food
126	108	72	29	18	7

Number of Passengers

NAME

SHARPEN YOUR SKILLS

Stem-and-Leaf Plots

Make a stem-and-leaf plot for the following data.

1. Compact Car Mileage Rating (miles per gallon)

27	40	31	33	32
31	25	35	40	28
32	36	37	28	40

2. Weekly Sales Video Cassettes

72	76	66	63	57	80
64	59	84	70	77	74
66	74	52	76	83	66

3. Heights of 7-12 Year Olds (in Inches)

62	61	46	53	50
51	47	59	53	48
60	53	52	48	52

Find the following for Exercise 1:

4. Range ____________ **5.** Mode ____________ **6.** Median ____________

Find the following for Exercise 2:

7. Range ____________ **8.** Mode ____________ **9.** Median ____________

Find the following for Exercise 3:

10. Range ____________ **11.** Mode ____________ **12.** Median ____________

NAME

SHARPEN YOUR SKILLS

Introducing Probability

Write the letters A - J on pieces of paper. Put the letters into a bag, and draw one without looking. After drawing, look at the letter and record it in the chart at the right. Replace the letter and repeat. Perform 30 trials of the experiment. Approximate each probability using your results.

	Tally and Number		Tally and Number
A		F	
B		G	
C		H	
D		I	
E		J	

1. *P* (B) ______

2. *P* (A, B, C, D, or E) ______

3. *P* (H, I, or J) ______

4. *P* (K) ______

5. *P* (F or G) ______

6. *P* (a vowel—A, E, or I) ______

7. *P* (a consonant—B, C D, F, G, H, or J) ______

Now perform 30 trials of the experiment using only the letters A, B, C, D. Approximate each probability using your results.

	A	B	C	D
Tally				
Number				

8. *P* (A) ______

9. *P* (B) ______

10. *P* (C) ______

11. *P* (D) ______

12. *P* (A or B) ______

Use after pages 480–481.

NAME ____________

SHARPEN YOUR SKILLS

Probability from Tables and Graphs

100 people rode different rides at a fair. Look at the table to see which rides they liked the best.

Rides at the Longview Fair	Favorite Ride
Rock-O-Plane	12
Tilt-a-Whirl	18
Merry-go-Round	21
Ferris Wheel	24
Roller Coaster	25

Approximate the probability that a person at the Longview Fair will

1. like the roller coaster best. ____________

2. like the rock-o-plane best. ____________

3. not like the Ferris wheel best. ____________

4. like neither the merry-go-round nor the tilt-a-whirl best. ____________

5. like the Ferris wheel best. ____________

6. like the rock-o-plane or the roller coaster best. ____________

Estimation If 2,000 people ride the rides at the fair, how many would you expect to

7. like the roller coaster best? ____________

8. like the Ferris wheel best? ____________

NAME

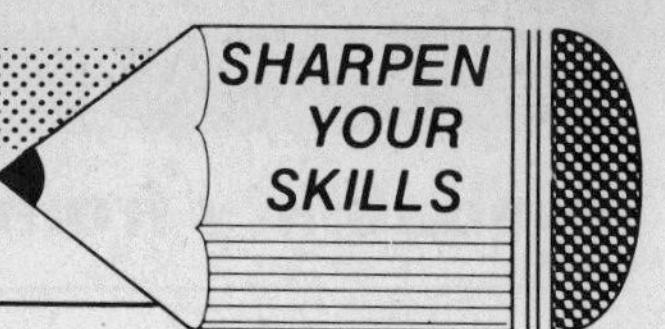

Theoretical Probability

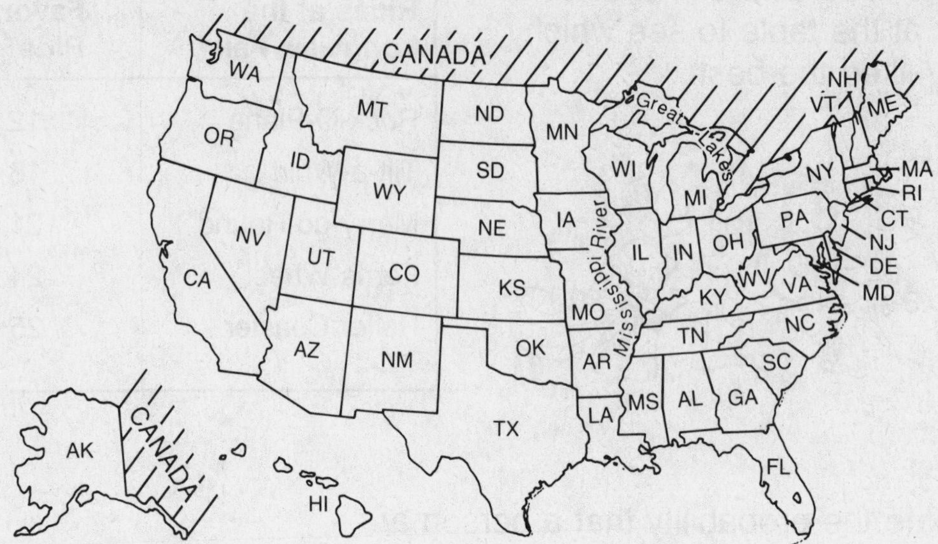

There are 50 slips of paper in a box. Each one has the abbreviation for one state on it. Find each theoretical probability if you draw one piece of paper from the box. **Remember** to count all the favorable outcomes.

1. *P* (the first letter of the abbreviation is a consonant)

____

2. *P* (the state shares a land border with Canada)

____

3. *P* (the state is west of the Mississippi River)

____

4. *P* (the state is surrounded by water)

____

5. *P* (the state touches one of the Great Lakes)

____

6. *P* (the first letter of the abbreviation is an A)

____

7. *P* (the state shares a border with Nevada)

____

8. *P* (the first letter of the abbreviation is an N)

____

NAME

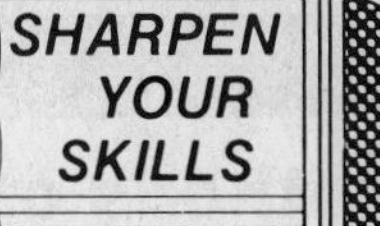

Draw a Diagram

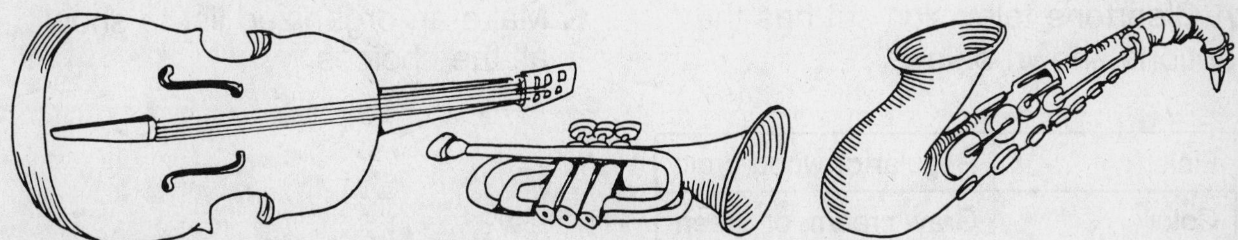

Draw a tree diagram to find the total number of choices in each exercise.

1. How many groups consisting of one piano player and one bass player can be formed from the following piano players and bass players?

Piano	Bass
Tony	Wayne
Luann	Stephanie
Jose	Nicole

2. The groups in Exercise 1 have a choice of two saxophone players: Amy or George. How many groups can be formed now?

NAME

SHARPEN YOUR SKILLS

Methods of Counting Choices

A Cleartone television set has the options shown below.

Finish	Regular or wood grain
Color	Gray, cream, or green
Remote control	Yes or no

1. Make an organized list to show all the choices.

2. Multiply to find the total number of choices.

3. How many choices are there if you want a green Cleartone?

4. How many choices are there if you want a wood grain Cleartone with remote control?

5. How many choices are there if you want a cream Cleartone without remote control?

Suppose a Cleartone came with the choices listed below.

Colors	15 colors
Stereo	Yes or no
CD player	Yes or no
Programming	Yes or no
Size	6 sizes
VCR	Yes or no

6. Multiply to find the total number of choices.

7. Multiply to find out how many choices there are for a Cleartone that is colored blue.

8. Multiply to find out how many choices there are for a cream Cleartone with a CD player.

NAME

SHARPEN YOUR SKILLS

Making Predictions

Seven students sold seeds to benefit the garden club. For each dollar's worth of seeds sold, a slip of paper with the student's name was put into a box. One student's name will be drawn to receive a prize. Use the chart to solve each problem.

Susan	$16
Michael	$ 8
Naomi	$18
Chris	$22
Byron	$23
Gretchen	$11
Philip	$22

1. Which student has the best chance to win?

2. Which student has the least chance to win?

3. What is the probability that Philip will win the prize?

4. What is the probability that Naomi will win the prize?

5. What is the probability that Chris or Susan will win the prize?

6. What is the probability that Gretchen will **not** win the prize?

7. What is the probability that Michael, Gretchen, or Susan will win the prize?

8. What is the probability that neither Naomi nor Byron will win the prize?

9. Which two students have an equal chance of winning?

Use after pages 494–495.

NAME

SHARPEN YOUR SKILLS

Collecting Data

Take a survey to find the favorite foods of students in your class.

1. Make a table to show your data.

2. You have $100 to spend on food for a school party. Use the data in your table to decide how much you would spend on foods from your survey. Spend a percent of the $100 equal to the percent of students choosing that food as their favorite.

3. Extend your survey. Have each student in your class survey 4 students from another class. Make a table to show your data.

4. Use the results of the survey in Exercise 3 to decide how to spend the $100 for the school party.

Critical Thinking Would the amounts in Exercise 2 be doubled if you started with $200? Why or why not?

NAME

SHARPEN YOUR SKILLS

Meaning of Integers

Write an integer to represent each situation.

1. Discount of $12 ____

2. Profit of $18 ____

3. Interest of $22 ____

4. Salary increase of $50 ____

5. 20° below zero ____

6. Sales decrease of $90 ____

7. Forward 5 feet ____

8. 75° above zero ____

9. Loss of $18 ____

10. Backward 2 feet ____

11. Bonus of $100 ____

12. Payroll deduction of $9 ____

13. Savings of $630 ____

14. Ditch depth of 8 feet ____

Write an integer for each situation.

15. Tim gained 7 pounds.

____

16. The temperature is 3° below zero.

____

17. Gail reached the airport 45 minutes before takeoff.

____

18. A snack was served 20 minutes after takeoff.

____

19. Kate bought a compact disk at a $20 discount.

____

20. The temperature in the theater was 68° above zero.

____

21. Al's cellar is 25 feet below the ground level.

____

22. Miss Gould received $18 in interest on her savings.

____

NAME

SHARPEN YOUR SKILLS

Integers on the Number Line

Give the integers for the lettered points listed below.

N G H A I D L E K F M

$^{-}10$ $^{-}8$ $^{-}6$ $^{-}4$ $^{-}2$ $^{-}1$ 0 $^{+}1$ $^{+}2$ $^{+}4$ $^{+}6$ $^{+}8$ $^{+}10$

1. E ________ **2.** F ________ **3.** A ________ **4.** D ________

5. H ________ **6.** G ________ **7.** I ________ **8.** K ________

Compare the integers. Use $<$ or $>$.

9. $^{+}19 \bigcirc ^{+}9$ **10.** $^{-}40 \bigcirc ^{-}3$ **11.** $^{+}51 \bigcirc ^{-}2$ **12.** $^{-}16 \bigcirc ^{+}3$

13. $^{+}80 \bigcirc ^{-}8$ **14.** $^{+}45 \bigcirc ^{+}4$ **15.** $^{-}12 \bigcirc ^{-}1$ **16.** $^{-}10 \bigcirc 0$

17. $^{-}83 \bigcirc ^{+}21$ **18.** $^{-}62 \bigcirc ^{-}14$ **19.** $^{-}21 \bigcirc ^{+}24$ **20.** $^{+}71 \bigcirc ^{-}71$

Arrange the integers in order from the least to the greatest.

21. $^{-}3$ $^{+}2$ $^{-}1$ ________

22. $^{+}1$ $^{+}3$ $^{-}1$ ________

23. $^{-}5$ $^{+}5$ $^{-}6$ ________

24. $^{-}7$ $^{+}2$ $^{+}4$ $^{-}1$ ________

25. $^{-}5$ $^{+}2$ $^{-}2$ $^{+}5$ ________

26. $^{-}1$ $^{+}6$ $^{-}3$ $^{+}5$ ________

27. $^{+}8$ $^{+}7$ $^{-}11$ $^{-}6$ ________

28. $^{-}9$ $^{+}11$ $^{-}2$ 0 ________

29. $^{-}56$ $^{-}65$ $^{-}78$ ________

Which temperature is colder?

30. 25° or 19° ________

31. $^{-}7$° or 7° ________

32. $^{-}13$° or 0° ________

NAME ____________________

SHARPEN YOUR SKILLS

Adding Integers

Find each sum. **Remember** to watch the signs.

1. $^{-}3 + {}^{+}7 =$ ________________

2. $^{+}3 + {}^{-}3 =$ ________________

3. $^{-}8 + {}^{+}4 =$ ________________

4. $^{-}8 + {}^{+}11 =$ ________________

5. $^{+}5 + {}^{-}6 =$ ________________

6. $^{+}16 + {}^{-}4 =$ ________________

7. $^{-}8 + {}^{+}23 =$ ________________

8. $^{+}25 + {}^{-}16 =$ ________________

9. $^{+}15 + {}^{-}23 =$ ________________

10. $^{+}24 + {}^{-}13 =$ ________________

11. $^{-}7 + {}^{+}20 =$ ________________

12. $^{+}3 + {}^{-}19 =$ ________________

13. $^{+}6 + {}^{-}18 =$ ________________

14. $^{+}5 + {}^{-}20 =$ ________________

15. $^{+}25 + {}^{-}11 =$ ________________

16. $^{-}22 + {}^{+}5 =$ ________________

17. $^{-}20 + {}^{+}25 =$ ________________

18. $^{+}24 + {}^{-}3 =$ ________________

19. $^{-}11 + {}^{+}2 =$ ________________

20. $^{-}15 + {}^{+}8 =$ ________________

21. $^{+}23 + {}^{-}3 =$ ________________

22. $^{-}17 + {}^{+}7 =$ ________________

23. $^{-}4 + {}^{+}12 =$ ________________

24. $^{-}1 + {}^{+}26 =$ ________________

Use integers to solve. **Remember** to label answers with a dollar sign ($) when writing money.

25. Tim had $52 in his checking account. He wrote a check for $55 and then made a deposit of $10. How much is in his account?

____

26. Eve's account was overdrawn by $12. The bank charged her $10. Then she deposited $90. How much is in her account?

____

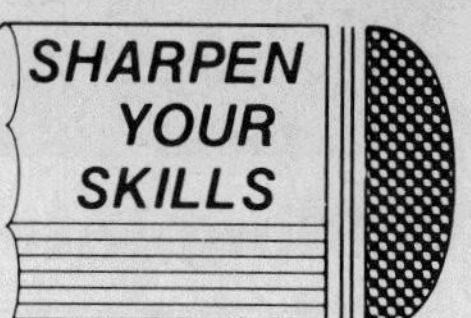

Subtracting Integers

What kind of room doesn't have walls, doors, or windows?

Find each difference. Then shade each shape where the answer is positive.

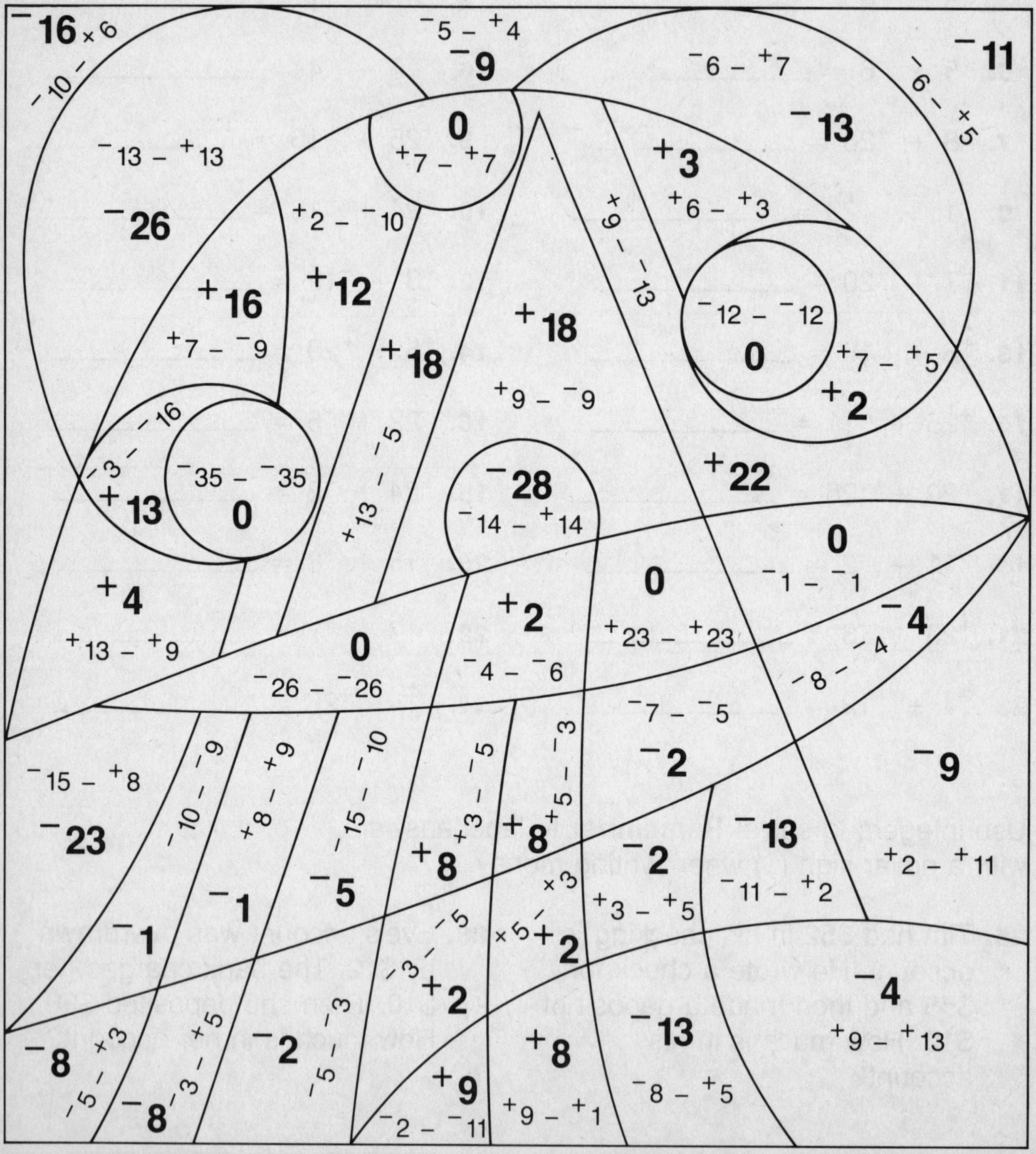

$^-10 - {}^+6$ $^-16$

$^-5 - {}^+4$ $^-9$

$^-6 - {}^+7$ $^-13$

$^-6 - {}^+5$ $^-11$

$^-13 - {}^+13$ $^-26$

$^+7 - {}^+7$ 0

$^+6 - {}^+3$ $^+3$

$^+9 - {}^-13$

$^+2 - {}^-10$ $^+12$

$^+7 - {}^-9$ $^+16$

$^+18$

$^+9 - {}^-9$ $^+18$

$^-12 - {}^-12$ 0

$^+7 - {}^+5$ $^+2$

$^-3 - {}^-16$ $^+13$

$^-35 - {}^-35$ 0

$^+13 - {}^-5$

$^-14 - {}^+14$ $^-28$

$^+22$

$^+13 - {}^+9$ $^+4$

$^-26 - {}^-26$ 0

$^-4 - {}^-6$ $^+2$

$^+23 - {}^+23$ 0

$^-1 - {}^-1$ 0

$^-8 - {}^-4$ $^-4$

$^-7 - {}^-5$ $^-2$

$^-9$

$^-15 - {}^+8$ $^-23$

$^-10 - {}^-9$ $^-1$

$^+8 - {}^+9$ $^-1$

$^-15 - {}^-10$ $^-5$

$^+3 - {}^-5$ $^+8$

$^+5 - {}^-3$ $^+8$

$^-2$

$^-11 - {}^+2$ $^-13$

$^+2 - {}^+11$

$^+3 - {}^+5$ $^-2$

$^-3 - {}^-5$ $^+2$

$^-5 - {}^+3$ $^+2$

$^-4$

$^-5 - {}^+3$ $^-8$

$^-3 - {}^+5$ $^-8$

$^-5 - {}^-3$ $^-2$

$^-2 - {}^-11$ $^+9$

$^+9 - {}^+1$ $^+8$

$^-8 - {}^+5$ $^-13$

$^+9 - {}^+13$

NAME

SHARPEN YOUR SKILLS

Multiplying and Dividing Integers

Multiply.

1. $20 \times {}^{-}2$ ______ **2.** ${}^{-}5 \times 30$ ______ **3.** $35 \times {}^{-}3$ ______ **4.** ${}^{-}22 \times {}^{-}4$ ______

5. ${}^{-}6 \times {}^{-}40$ ______ **6.** 15×20 ______ **7.** ${}^{-}12 \times 8$ ______ **8.** ${}^{-}20 \times {}^{-}40$ ______

Compute each of these products.

9. ${}^{-}6({}^{-}20)$ ______ **10.** $(8)\ {}^{-}60$ ______ **11.** ${}^{-}7({}^{-}80)({}^{-}1)$ ______ **12.** ${}^{-}6(40)(6)$ ______

Divide.

13. $54 \div {}^{-}9$ ______ **14.** ${}^{-}55 \div {}^{-}5$ ______ **15.** $168 \div {}^{-}12$ ______ **16.** ${}^{-}156 \div 39$ ______

17. $0 \div {}^{-}5$ ______ **18.** ${}^{-}63 \div {}^{-}1$ ______ **19.** $63 \div 7$ ______ **20.** ${}^{-}770 \div 10$ ______

21. If an elevator goes up 3 floors and down 2 every minute, how far will it go in 5 minutes?

______

22. If the elevator begins on the ninth floor, where will it be in 10 minutes?

______

Use after pages 518–521.

NAME

SHARPEN YOUR SKILLS

Choose an Operation

Use integers to solve these problems.
Remember to watch the signs.

1. What was the total amount of change in temperature for the six days shown? What was the average amount of change?

Day	1	2	3	4	5	6
Change	$^{-}6$	$^{+}5$	$^{+}1$	$^{+}5$	$^{-}1$	$^{+}2$

2. What was the total amount of change in temperature for the six days shown? What was the average amount of change?

Day	1	2	3	4	5	6
Change	$^{-}3$	$^{+}7$	$^{-}2$	$^{-}1$	$^{+}5$	$^{+}6$

3. The chart below shows the temperatures for one week in Brattleboro, Vermont. Find the average change in these temperatures for the week.

Day	S	M	T	W	T	F	S
Temp. °F	42	48	37	32	39	41	30

4. The chart below shows the temperatures for the same week in Portland, Maine. What was the average change in these temperatures for the week?

Day	S	M	T	W	T	F	S
Temp. °F	30	35	25	16	18	23	12

NAME

SHARPEN YOUR SKILLS

Locating Points in Four Quadrants

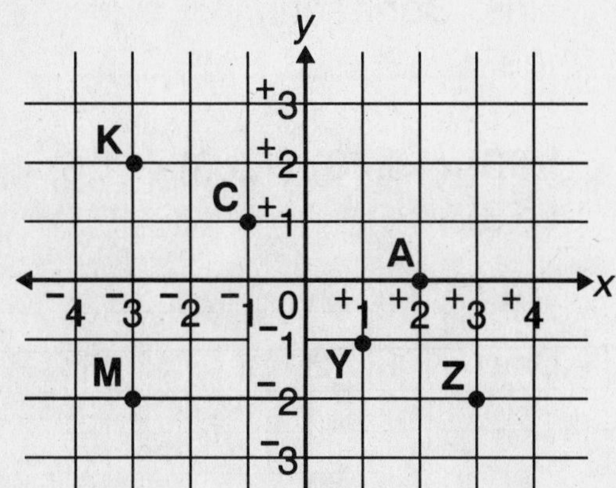

Tell which point is located by each ordered pair in the graph above.

1. $(^+2, 0)$ ____ **2.** $(^-3, ^+2)$ ____

3. $(^-3, ^-2)$ ____ **4.** $(^+1, ^-1)$ ____

Give the ordered pair that locates each point in the graph above.

5. B ________ **6.** N ________

7. L ________ **8.** V ________

Use Exercises 9–24 to help finish the picture below. On the grid, make a dot for each ordered pair. Connect the dots in order.

9. $(^+3, ^+3)$ **10.** $(^+4, ^+3)$ **11.** $(^+5, ^+2)$ **12.** $(^+5, ^+1)$

13. $(^+6, 0)$ **14.** $(^+9, 0)$ **15.** $(^+9, ^-1)$ **16.** $(^+8, ^-2)$

17. $(^-6, ^-2)$ **18.** $(^-7, ^-1)$ **19.** $(^-7, ^+1)$ **20.** $(^-5, ^+2)$

21. $(^-3, ^+2)$ **22.** $(^-2, ^+1)$ **23.** $(^-1, ^+1)$ **24.** $(^+1, ^+1)$

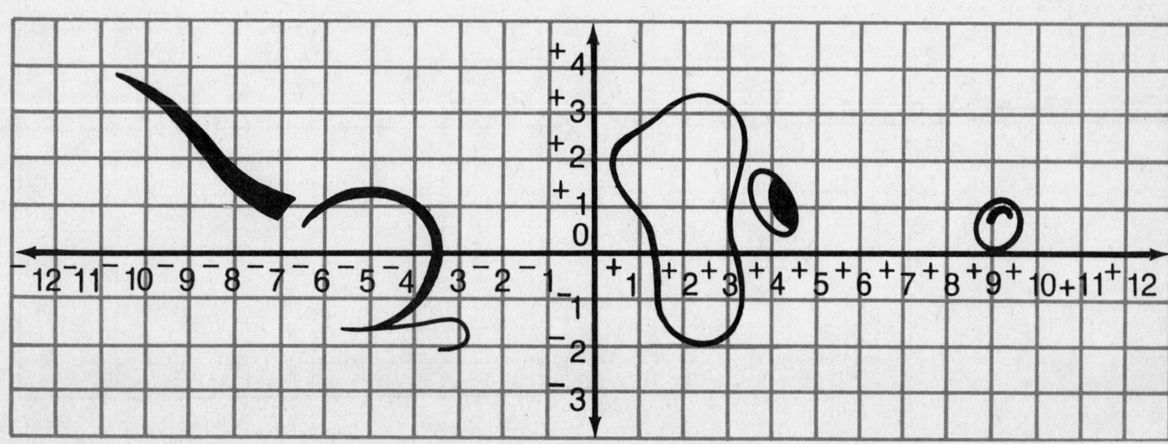

SHARPEN YOUR SKILLS

Use Data from a Graph

Draw each figure by plotting the given points and connecting them in order. Then flip the figure over the *y*-axis. Connect the points of the flipped figure using dotted lines.

1. $(1,0)$ $(4,4)$ $(7,0)$ $(4,{}^-4)$ $(1,0)$

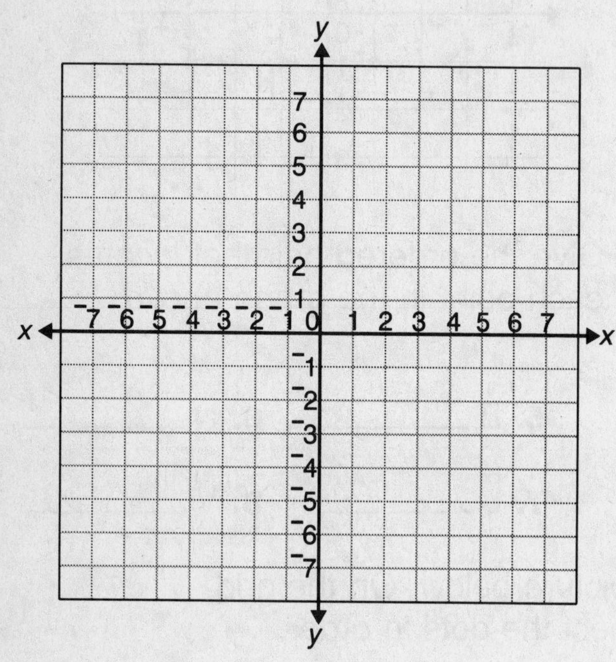

2. $({}^-1,{}^-3)$ $({}^-5,{}^-3)$ $({}^-5,6)$ $({}^-1,6)$ $({}^-1,{}^-3)$

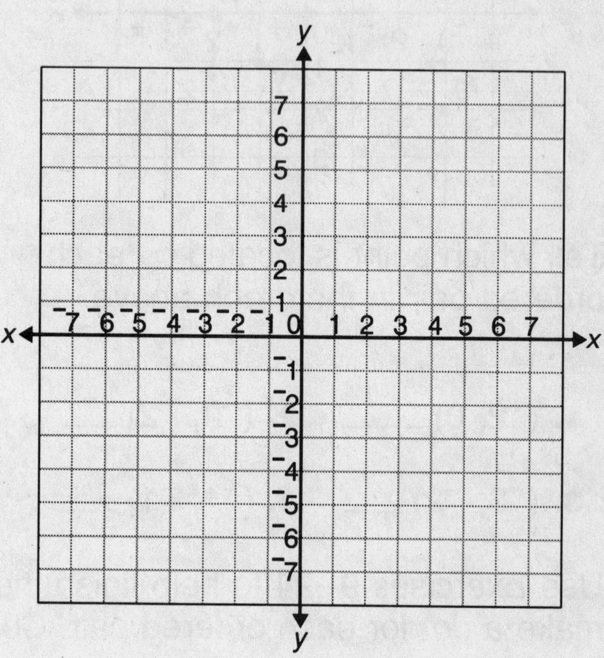

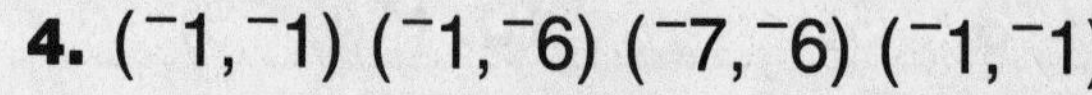

3. $(1,{}^-2)$ $(6,{}^-5)$ $(1,{}^-5)$ $(1,{}^-2)$

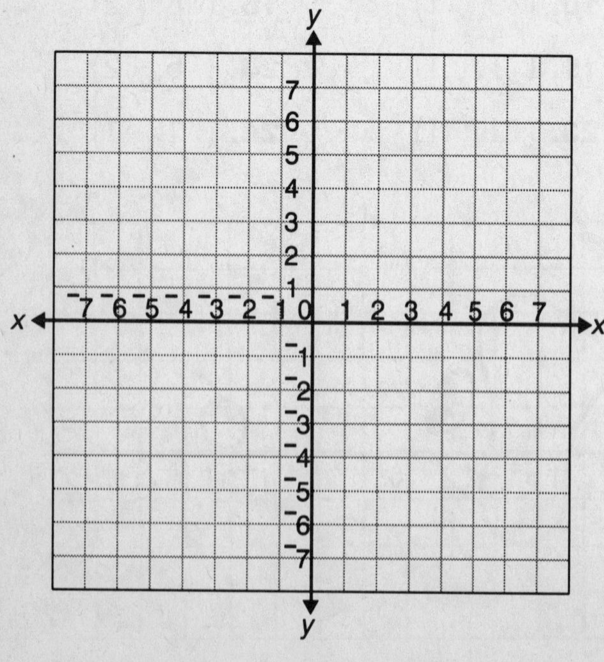

4. $({}^-1,{}^-1)$ $({}^-1,{}^-6)$ $({}^-7,{}^-6)$ $({}^-1,{}^-1)$

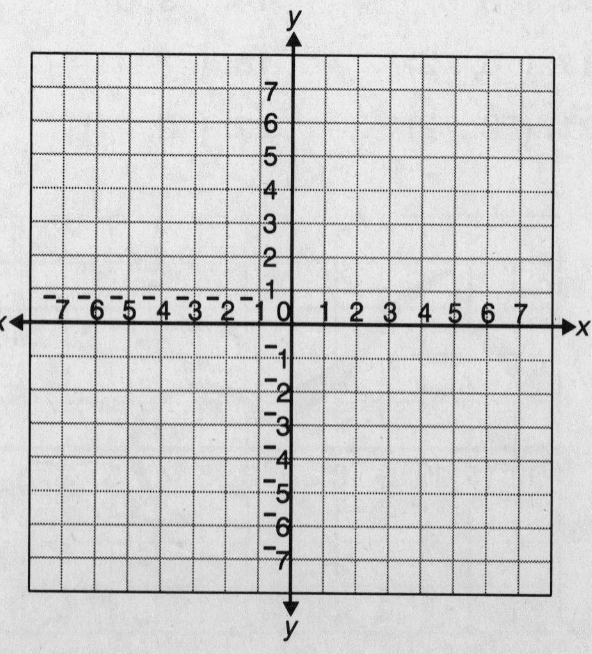

Use after pages 528–529.

NAME

SHARPEN YOUR SKILLS

Graphing in Four Quadrants

Complete each table and graph the rule.

1. $y = x + {}^{+}3$

x	+4	+2	+0	−2
y	+7			

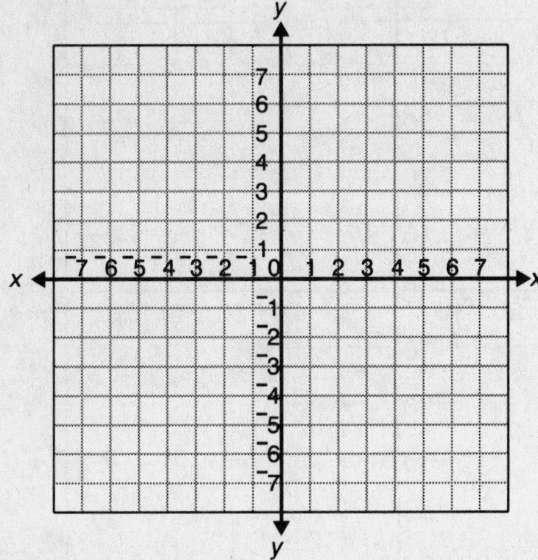

2. $y = x - {}^{-}5$

x	+1	−3	−5	−7
y				

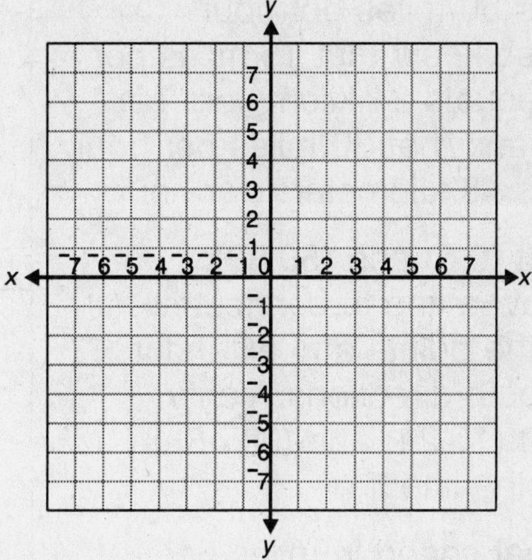

3. $y = x + {}^{-}4$

x	+7	+2	+1	0
y				

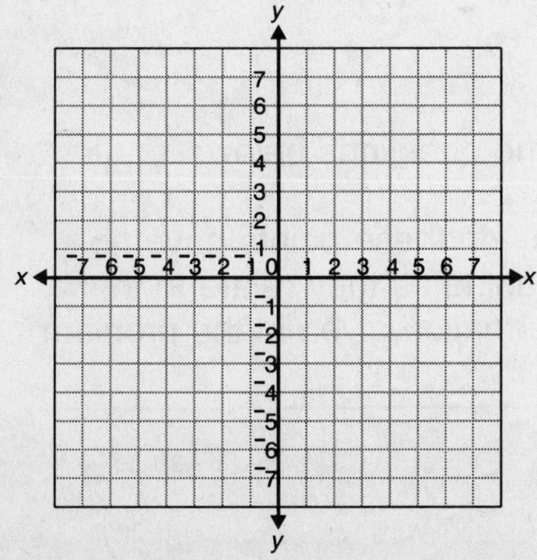

4. $y = x - {}^{+}1$

x	+5	+3	−1	−4
y				

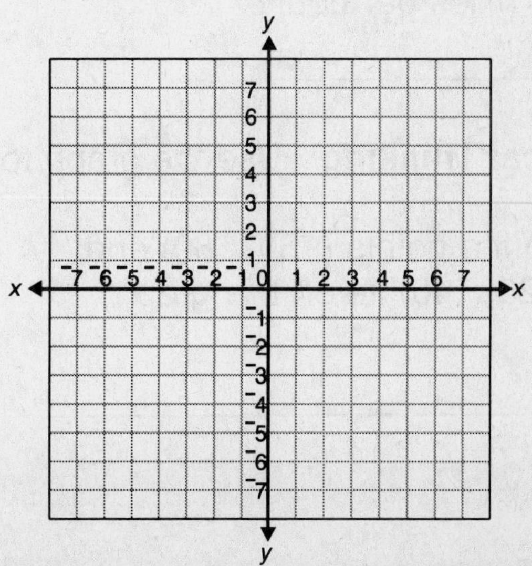

NAME

SHARPEN YOUR SKILLS

Make a Graph

The speedometer in the car Mr. Jones drove in England measured kilometers. He wanted to know how kilometers per hour compared with miles per hour. He knew that 80 kilometers per hour equals 50 miles per hour. He also knew that 15 miles per hour equals 24 kilometers per hour, and that 30 miles per hour equals 48 kilometers per hour.

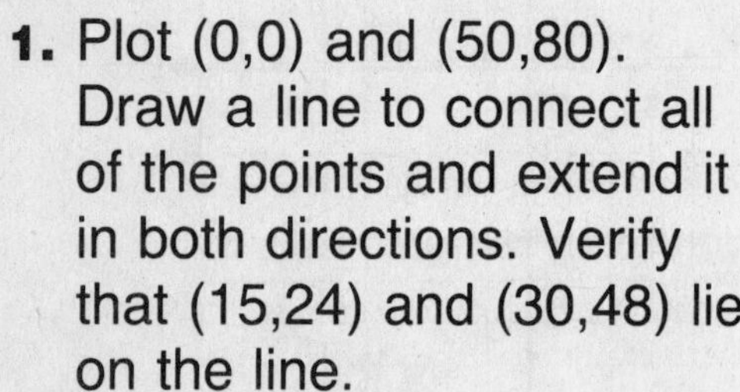

1. Plot (0,0) and (50,80). Draw a line to connect all of the points and extend it in both directions. Verify that (15,24) and (30,48) lie on the line.

2. What speed in miles per hour corresponds to 40 kilometers per hour?

____

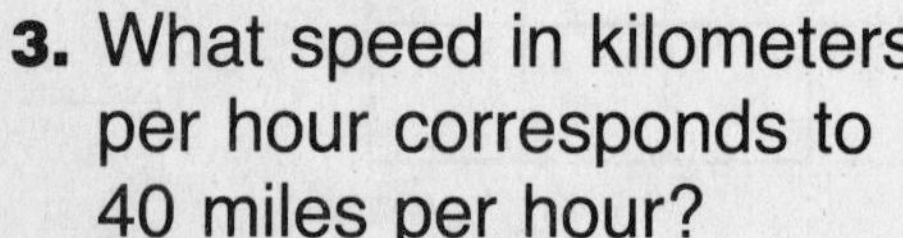

3. What speed in kilometers per hour corresponds to 40 miles per hour?

____

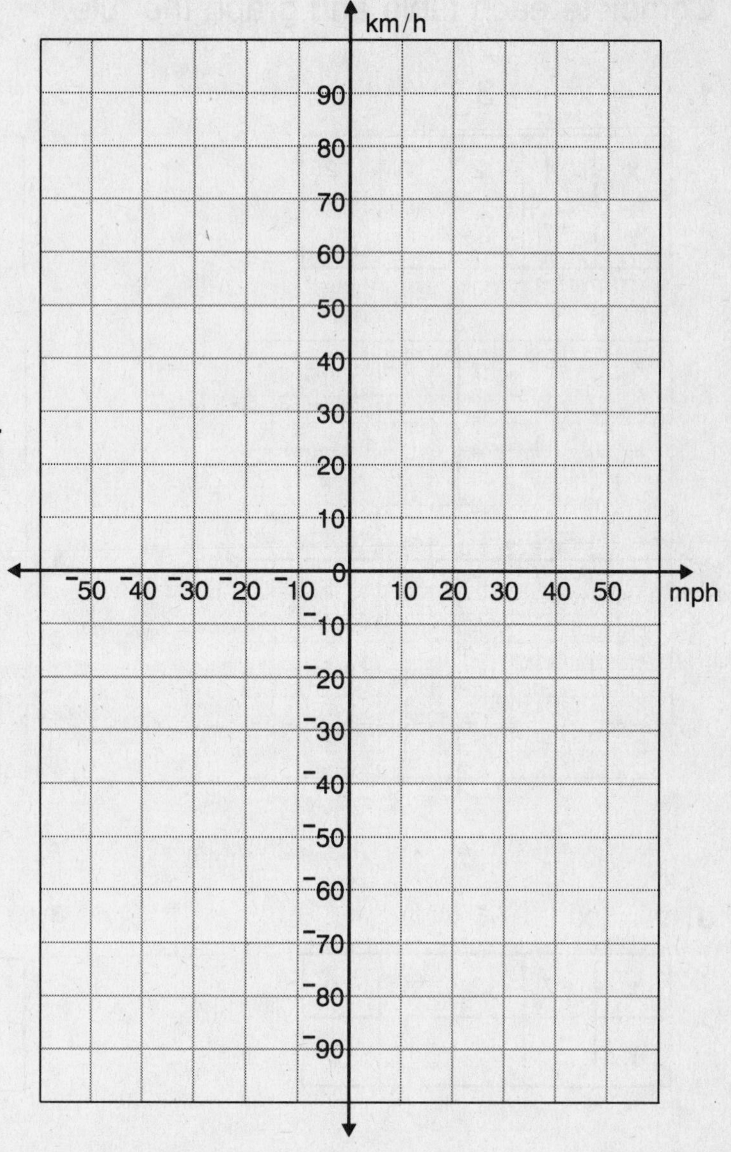

Critical Thinking Use the graph to answer the questions below.

4. Do the points ($^{-}$50, $^{-}$80) and ($^{-}$25, $^{-}$40) lie on this graph?

____

5. Why do these points have no meaning as they relate to the information given in the problem?

____

Use after pages 532–533.